CW01338038

MAX'S

Digital SAT Grammar

Essential Guide and Drill

Second Edition

Max's SAT Prep Series:

- **Max's Digital SAT Reading: Essential Guide and Drill**
- **Max's Digital SAT Grammar: Essential Guide and Drill**
- **Max's Digital SAT Practice Test #1: Reading and Writing**
- **Max's Digital SAT Practice Test #2: Reading and Writing**

Max's Digital SAT Grammar: Essential Guide and Drill

[2nd Edition]

ISBN: 979-8-9886526-4-9

INTRODUCTION

Welcome to the second edition of *Max's Digital SAT Grammar: Essential Guide and Drill.*

This specialized guidebook is divided into two main parts.

The first part is the **Essential Guide**, which thoroughly explains the core grammar concepts tested on the SAT. It covers everything from the basics of sentence structure to the intricacies of punctuation use, verb tense consistency, and more. Each section is structured with clear, concise explanations and illustrative examples, designed to be accessible to all learners, no matter your current level of understanding.

The second part is the **Drill**. Here, we offer a variety of practice questions that simulate actual Digital SAT questions. These exercises are specifically tailored to mimic the SAT testing environment, helping you become familiar with the types and structures of questions you will face on the exam. Comprehensive explanations are provided for each question, so you can understand the rationale behind the correct answers and learn from any mistakes you might make.

In this updated second edition, we've made significant improvements by correcting ambiguous instruction explanations. This ensures that all guidance is clear and precise, allowing you to study more effectively and confidently.

I believe in being thoroughly prepared rather than underinformed. That's why I've analyzed not only the Digital SAT but also its predecessor, the redesigned SAT. When the College Board introduced the redesigned SAT in 2016, I examined the practice tests and continued analyzing subsequent exams. Through this ongoing effort, I compiled key grammatical concepts that I knew would be essential for my students to master.

Beyond the commonly tested topics, I've included some challenging grammatical concepts that appeared only occasionally on the redesigned SAT yet often prove difficult for students to grasp or find clear explanations for. For instance, "ellipsis" was tested in May 2017, "semicolons" for lists in December 2017, and "asyndeton" in March 2021. While "semicolons" for lists appeared only once on the redesigned SAT, it has become more common on the Digital SAT.

"I'm a great believer in luck, and I find the harder I work, the more I have of it."

- Thomas Jefferson

In short, every example question and sentence in this book is modeled on actual SAT questions from 2016 to the present, ensuring that you are well-prepared for the exam.

When analyzing the questions, I categorize them by type and further organize questions within each category. I then delve into each type to identify recurring patterns.

For example, I used the College Board Question Bank to analyze all the "Rhetorical Synthesis" questions. I checked the question stems that say "The student wants to ...", then sorted the questions that ask the same task. I noticed that for questions that ask about similarity, the correct answer often contains words like "neither," "both," "likewise," or "like."

The ultimate goal of this book is to help you achieve your highest possible score on the SAT. Remember, this isn't just about passing the test—it's about understanding English grammar deeply and using it effectively, which will serve you well in college and beyond.

So, whether you're just starting your SAT preparation or looking to hone your grammar skills further, *Max's Digital SAT Grammar: Essential Guide and Drill* is your trusted companion. Use it diligently, revisit sections as needed, and don't hesitate to reach out if you have any questions or need additional support.

Get ready to conquer the SAT with confidence!

Max (Byung Seuk) Kim
Seoul, Korea
November 2024

Table of Contents

Chapter 6. Punctuation

Chapter 7. Question Type Approach

Chapter 8. Four Test Sets

Chapter 9. Answers

1

PARTS OF SPEECH

- ❐ NOUN
- ❐ PRONOUN
- ❐ ADJECTIVE
- ❐ ADVERB
- ❐ PREPOSITION
- ❐ VERB
- ❐ CONJUNCTION
- ❐ INTERJECTION

NOUN

WHAT IS A NOUN?

A noun is a word that names a person, place, thing, animal, or idea.

LESSON 1 **A noun can function as a subject, object, or complement in a sentence.**

EXAMPLE

- A bicycle (subj.) is a vehicle (comp.) with two wheels (obj.).
- A boy (subj.) kick the ball (obj.).

LESSON 2 **Nouns can be classified as either countable or uncountable.**

EXAMPLE

Countable Nouns: Refer to items that can be counted and have singular and plural forms.

Singular: a boy
Plural: boys

Uncountable Nouns: Refer to substances or concepts that cannot be counted individually and usually do not have a plural form.

Example: furniture

Note: Uncountable nouns generally take singular verbs.

LESSON 3 **Nouns can also be categorized into different types.**

EXAMPLE

1. **Common Nouns:** General names for persons, places, things, or ideas.

pen	desk	person	bird

2. **Collective Nouns:** Words that refer to a group treated as a single entity.

family	herd	pack	couple

3. Material Nouns: Names of materials or substances.			
water	air	money	sand

4. Abstract Nouns: Names of qualities, concepts, or ideas that cannot be perceived by the senses.			
beauty	freedom	courage	honesty

5. Proper Nouns: Specific names of particular persons, places, or things; always capitalized.			
February	Fiji	James	Christmas

Additional Tips:
Some nouns can be both countable and uncountable depending on the context.

Example: Light (uncountable when referring to illumination; countable when referring to light sources).

Collective nouns may take singular or plural verbs based on whether the group acts as one unit or as individuals.

Singular: The team is winning.
Plural: The team are arguing among themselves.

NOUN DRILL

Answers are provided on page196.

INSTRUCTION

Underline all the nouns in the following sentences and mark S for singular(including uncountable nouns) and P for plural above each noun.

1

Nature's splendor has captivated me for my entire life. It's breathtaking to see the mighty mountains with their soaring summits. The vibrant flowers that adorn the meadows make me happy. I can't help but be in awe of the calm of the flowing water as I stroll along the riverbank. The chirping of birds in the sky contributes to nature's melody. The limbs of each tree in the forest reach upward to tell a different tale. I am constantly in awe of nature's marvels, from the tiniest pebble to the largest waterfall.

2

I like experimenting with different recipes in my kitchen. I made the decision to make chocolate-chip cookies today. I took great care when measuring the flour, sugar, and butter. The perfume of vanilla extract permeated the room as I stirred the dough. As I melted the chocolate chips into the mixture, I added them. I then rolled the dough into small balls and put them on a baking sheet. The cookies started to become golden brown after a few minutes in the oven. I couldn't wait to share the batch's twelve delectable delights with my family and friends. Baking is more than simply a pastime; it's a great way to make appetizing treats and cheer up other people.

3

Sarah is a voracious antique book collector. Each book on her shelves tells a different story and is rich with gems. She admires the elaborate pictures and meticulously maintained texts as she turns the pages. Sarah takes pride in the range of genres that are represented in her collection, which includes historical biographies and classic novels. Each new item she adds to her collection makes her happy and excited. Whenever people come over, they are in awe of the enormous variety of literary treasures that line her bookcases. Sarah's love of reading and the pleasure it offers her is evident in her passion for book collecting.

NOTE BOX

Defining the types of nouns above is not important, but it is essential to know whether the noun is singular or plural.

PRONOUN

WHAT IS A PRONOUN?

A pronoun is a word that is used to substitute for a noun.

LESSON 1

The noun or noun phrase that a pronoun refers to is called its antecedent.

EXAMPLE

- I bought a *car*, and my wife really liked *it*.

EXPLANATION The noun *car* is the antecedent for the pronoun *it*.

LESSON 2

Personal pronouns refer to specific persons or things and change form based on their grammatical case: subjective, possessive, or objective. The pronouns it (singular) and they (plural) are used to replace nonhuman nouns.

EXAMPLE

	Subjective Case	Possessive Case	Objective Case	Possessive Pronoun
1st person singular	I	my	me	mine
1st person plural	we	our	us	ours
2nd person plural	you	your	you	yours
3rd person singular	he/she	his/her	him/her	his/hers
3rd person plural	they	their	them	theirs
Nonhuman	it	its	it	---

LESSON 3

Example sentences using personal pronouns

EXAMPLE

Subjective Case	Possessive Case & Possessive Pronoun	Objective Case

- Eugene and ***I*** were roommates back in our freshman year.
- ***We*** always had a good time until ***he*** transferred to another college.

Subjective Case	**Possessive Case & Possessive Pronoun**	Objective Case

- Although ***my computer*** is more expensive, ***theirs***(their computer) offers better performance and advanced features.
- Although ***my computers*** are more expensive, ***theirs***(their computers) offer better performance and advanced features.

Subjective Case	Possessive Case & Possessive Pronoun	**Objective Case**

- The conflicts between my brother and ***me*** are not a big deal.
- Since Chris had no money to buy food, Alex lent ***him*** money.

LESSON 4

Reflexive pronouns are used when the subject and the object of a sentence are the same or to emphasize the subject.

EXAMPLE

myself	yourself	ourselves	herself	himself	them-selves	itself

Refer back

- Narcissus loved ***himself.***

Emphasize

- I ***myself*** hit the ball.

LESSON 5

The pronoun *it* serves multiple roles in English.

EXAMPLE

Roles	Example Sentences
Referring *it* Replaces a noun or a clause	Although initially this ***movement*** was meant only for the masses, ***it*** quickly spread throughout all of Chinese society. Many said ***that Pocahontas is fat***, but I did not believe ***it***.
Impersonal Pronoun *it* Used as a subject when referring to *time*, *distance*, *weather*, or general situations. Here, *it* does not have a specific antecedent.	Because ***it*** was raining, I bought an umbrella. *It* is important to understand the structure of molecules. *It* is five o'clock. *It* is 10 miles to the nearest gas station.
Dummy Subject *it* Acts as a placeholder when the real subject or object is an infinitive phrase or a clause.	***It*** is essential *to* ***understand the structure of molecules.*** Advancements in technology make ***it*** challenging ***for individuals to secure job without pursuing higher education.*** ***It*** is important ***that I exercise as soon as possible.***

LESSON 6

Demonstrative pronouns point to and identify a specific person, object, or idea, indicating its proximity to the speaker or listener.

EXAMPLE

this	that	these	those

- *That* is my new car.
- I won the first prize in the competition, and ***that*** made me happy.
- The color of the shoes clashes with ***that*** of the suit.

LESSON 7

Indefinite pronouns refer to nonspecific persons or objects. Subject-verb agreement can be tricky because some indefinite pronouns are always singular, some always plural, and some can be both.

EXAMPLE

Singular	much, any, each, either, neither, anything, anyone, anybody, something, someone, somebody, every, everyone, nothing, nobody, another, everything • *Everyone* needs to sleep.
Plural	both, many, other • ***Both*** of my brothers like to exercise every day.
Both	all, most, some, half, none • ***All*** of the ***water*** is drained. • ***All*** of the ***classmates*** have turned into zombies.

EXPLANATION

When ***all*** refers to the uncountable noun ***water***, a singular verb is used; however, when ***all*** refers to the plural countable noun ***classmates***, a plural verb is used.

LESSON 8

Relative pronouns are conjunctions that lead modifying clauses.

EXAMPLE

who	whom	that	which	whose

I like to practice Pilates, ***which*** is a form of exercise ***that*** focuses on developing strength, flexibility, and control of the body through a series of precise movements and breathing techniques.

PRONOUN DRILL 1

Answers are provided on page 197.

INSTRUCTION

Underline the pronouns in the following sentences. If there is an antecedent that a pronoun refers to, then you should indicate this relationship by drawing a line between the pronoun and the antecedent.

1 Sulfur dioxide causes acid rain, which damages crops and forests, and contributes to respiratory problems in humans and animals, particularly in those with asthma or other lung diseases.

2 Juliet met Romeo, who is the old foe of her family, and she fell deeply in love with him, despite the longstanding feud between their families.

3 Art critics who write for mainstream publications often need to balance their own personal opinions about an artwork with the broader public's perception and understanding of it.

4 Some carried briefcases, others had backpacks slung over their shoulder.

5 Superman, whose story dates back to the late 1930s, is known for his extraordinary powers and commitment to justice.

PRONOUN DRILL 2

Answers are provided on page 197~198.

INSTRUCTION **Choose the correct pronoun.**

1 The masterpiece painting "Mona Lisa" by Leonardo da Vinci is celebrated for its artistic brilliance, but we must remember that (his/our) creation was made possible through the use of various techniques and skills employed by da Vinci and other artists of the Renaissance era.

2 Susan has captivated readers with her compelling storytelling and vivid imagination. She finds inspiration for (her/their) creative works in a variety of experiences and sources.

3 Ecologists have studied how certain plants can close (itself/themselves) up in response to touch or disturbances, protecting their delicate flowers or leaves from potential harm.

4 Linda has been a driving force behind several successful social initiatives. Her dedication and passion for making a positive change in the world have motivated others to join (her/their) cause.

5 The renowned artists Pablo Picasso and Georges Braque are often credited with the invention of Cubism, but (their/its) development was influenced by the artistic experiments of predecessors such as Paul Cézanne and Henri Matisse.

6 Researchers have discovered that certain types of orchids have the ability to change (them/themselves) in response to environmental conditions, allowing them to adapt to different pollinators.

7 As a candidate for the position, what qualities and skills make (me/myself) a strong fit for this role?

8 Researcher Maria Garcia argues that public health campaigns promoting regular exercise can yield positive outcomes, particularly when these campaigns provide individuals with options: for example, a study showed that gym attendance increased by 30% after individuals were asked whether (they/he) wanted to join fitness classes.

9 When it comes to personal growth and development, certain strategies and practices have helped (me/myself) overcome challenges and achieve success.

10 Scientists have found that certain species of lizards can detach (them/themselves) from their tails as a defense mechanism, distracting predators while the lizards make a quick escape.

11 Environmental organizations stress that awareness campaigns on sustainable transportation can have a significant impact, particularly when these campaigns emphasize the importance of eco-friendly options: for example, a town experienced a rise in bicycle ridership after residents were asked whether (they/it) would consider cycling for short distances.

ADJECTIVE

WHAT IS AN ADJECTIVE?

An adjective is a word, phrase, or clause that modifies a noun.

LESSON 1 **Most adjectives end with -able, -ive, -ful, -ic, -ous.**

EXAMPLE

- Alex drives ***a comfortable*** car.
- Chicago has ***many iconic*** buildings.

EXPLANATION Even articles ***a*** and ***the*** are regarded as adjectives.

LESSON 2 **Some adjectives are confused with adverbs because they end with -ly.**

EXAMPLE

friendly costly timely orderly likely

- Please finish this project in a ***timely*** manner.

LESSON 3 **General adjectives directly modify nouns**

EXAMPLE

- A ***wise*** man built his house on the rock.

LESSON 4 **Quantitative adjectives show quantity**

EXAMPLE

- John does not have ***much*** time.
- ***Many*** books are available in digital format.

LESSON 5

Indefinite adjectives do not refer to any specific person, thing, or amount.

EXAMPLE

Some	Most	All	Other

- Almost ***all*** elementary students have smartphones.
- ***Other*** information is needed to make a proper decision.

LESSON 6

An adjective can be expressed as a phrase or clause.

EXAMPLE

- The butcher ***with a boning knife*** looks professional.
- The butcher ***who always grinds his knife at noon*** looks happy.

ADVERB

WHAT IS AN ADVERB

An adverb modifies a verb, an adjective, another adverb, or a whole sentence.

LESSON 1

It is essential to know what the modifiers are because you sometimes need to cross out modifiers to spot the subject and verb correctly.

EXAMPLE

Generally, truly great singers regularly practice singing at the company's studio to continuously improve their vocal skills before performing on stage.

What answers the following questions are *adverbs*.

- Under what circumstances? **Generally**
- To what extent? **truly**
- How often? **regularly**
- Where? **at the company's studio**
- Why? **to continuously improve their vocal skills**
- How? **continuously**
- When? **before performing on stage**

LESSON 2 Use adverbs for action verbs and adjectives for linking and be verbs

EXAMPLE

- Alex drives (action v.) a car comfortably (adv.).
- Many of the buildings in Chicago are (be v.) beautiful (adj.).
- This apple tastes (linking v.) fantastic (adj.).
- I tasted (action v.) the apple cautiously (adv.).

EXPLANATION **Depending on the context, linking verbs can be used as action verbs.**

EXAMPLE **The following example is what the SAT question about adjectives and adverbs would look like.**

The intense heat causes water to evaporate ______ the surface of the lake than from the surrounding soil.

A) quicker from

B) more quickly from

C) most quickly from

D) quickly from

EXPLANATION The word should modify ***evaporate***; therefore, we need an adverb ***quickly***. There is ***than*** later in the sentence so we need a comparative form. The answer is **B**.

ADJECTIVE AND ADVERB DRILL

Answers are provided on page 199.

INSTRUCTION

Underline all the adjectives and adverbs in the following sentences and mark ADJ for adjectives and ADV for adverbs.

1. She sang a beautiful song.

2. He ran quickly to catch the bus.

3. The cake tasted deliciously sweet.

4. The lazy cat slept peacefully on the windowsill.

5. The sun shone brightly on the sandy beach.

PREPOSITION

WHAT IS A PREPOSITION

Prepositions are words that show the relationship between a noun or pronoun and other words in a sentence. They often indicate direction, location, time, or introduce an object.

LESSON 1

Prepositions are always part of a prepositional phrase, which consists of the preposition followed by its object (a noun or pronoun).

EXAMPLE

- The US government is *of the people, by the people,* and *for the people.*
- Exposure *to nature* has been shown to have a positive impact *on mental health*, improving overall well-being and reducing symptoms *of anxiety and depression.*

EXPLANATION In each example, the preposition is followed by a noun or noun phrase, forming a prepositional phrase.

LESSON 2

Prepositional phrases function as modifiers in a sentence, acting either as adjectives or adverbs. They are not essential to form complete sentences but provide additional information.

EXAMPLE

- I slept <u>on the grass.</u> (**adv. phrase**)
- I slept. (Sentence is still complete without the prepositional phrase)
- The cup <u>on the table</u> (**adj. phrase**) has cracks.
- The cup has cracks. (Sentence is still complete without the prepositional phrase)

LESSON 3

Common Prepositions

EXAMPLE

In	On	At	Since	By	Until
Before	Prior to	After	For	During	Over
Throughout	Within	To	From	Through	Into
Out of	Across	Between	Among	Within	Above
Over	Under	Below	Beside	Next to	Along
Due to	Because of	Owing to	Thanks to	Despite	In spite of
With	Without	Except (for)	In addition to	Besides	Instead of
About	Regarding	Concerning	As to	Pertinent to	Pertaining to
By	Like	Unlike	As		

LESSON 4

Some words can function either as prepositions or subordinating conjunctions, depending on how they are used in a sentence.

EXAMPLE

- I can't go to bed <u>until</u> (conj.) I finish this book.
- I can't go to bed <u>until</u> (prep.) 3 o'clock.

PREPOSITION DRILL

Answers are provided on page 199.

INSTRUCTION **Put parentheses around prepositional phrases.**

1 If radioactive water from a damaged power plant is released, it can have serious consequences for human health and the environment, depending on the amount and type of radioactive material released and the location of the release.

2 The potential health risks of exposure to radioactive water include radiation sickness, cancer, genetic mutations, and other health problems.

3 Additionally, the release of radioactive water can also have long-term environmental impacts, such as contamination of soil, water, and food sources, as well as harm to wildlife and marine ecosystems.

4 It's important to note that the consequences of a release of radioactive water can be severe and long-lasting.

5 Therefore, it's crucial to take all necessary measures to prevent such incidents and to properly manage radioactive waste to minimize the risk of such accidents in the future.

VERB

WHAT IS A VERB

Verbs describe an action, condition, or state of being.

LESSON 1

When the subject of a sentence is singular and the verb is in the present tense, you need to add -s, -es, or -ies to the base form of the verb.

EXAMPLE

- <u>The Mississippi River</u> ***flows*** (**sing.**) southward from its source at Lake Itasca in Minnesota, through several states, and eventually empties into the Gulf of Mexico.
- The <u>stars</u> ***have*** (**plr.**) inspired countless poets, writers, and artists, and ***continue*** (**plr.**) to captivate us with their beauty and mystery.

LESSON 2

All verbs have 3 forms: Present, Past, Past Participle. With these forms, verbs can convey various tenses. "-ed" or "–d" is placed at the end of the regular verb; however, <u>irregular verbs</u> do not follow the "regular" pattern.

EXAMPLE

	Present	Past	Past Participle
Regular	work	worked	have worked
Irregular	eat	ate	have eaten

Below are the ways that irregular verbs change their forms.

Type	Pattern	Feature
cast	cast – cast – have cast	All forms are same.
bring	bring – brought – have brought	Last two are same.
break	break – broke – have broken	past + n = past participle
swim	swim – swam – have swum	change in vowel sound
eat	eat- ate- have eaten	All three forms are different.
show	show – showed – have showed/ shown	Past participle forms have both forms.
spill	spill- spilled/spilt – have spilled/ spilt	past and past participle forms
lie	lie – lied – have lied lie – lay – have laid	same original forms but the meaning differs

LESSON 3

Helping verbs are used before main verbs to form different tenses, moods, or voices.

EXAMPLE

Category	Helping Verbs				
Pure helping verbs	will/would	shall/should	can/could	may/might	must
Semi-helping verbs	need dare	used to need tor	ought to have to	had better would rather	
Be verbs	am	is	are	was	were
Have verbs	have	has	had		

RULES

1> Do not use two pure helping verbs together before a main verb.

- I ***will can*** do the work. (X)
- I ***will*** do the work. (O)
- I ***can*** do the work. (O)

2> Pure helping verbs remain in their base form, regardless of the subject.

- John ***musts*** do the work. (X)
- John ***must*** do the work. (O)

Common Mistake: When "need" and "dare" are used as helping verbs, they stay in their base form.

- John ***needs*** not do the work. (X)
- John ***need*** not do the work. (O)

3> The main verb following a pure helping verb must be in its base form.

- One of the many islands in Korea, Dokdo ***must is*** the one that has the most beautiful sunset. (X)
- One of the many islands in Korea, Dokdo ***must be*** the one that has the most beautiful sunset. (O)

LESSON 4

Helping verbs assist the main verb in expressing the following: intensity or emphasis, indicating tense, changing the voice from active to passive, and conveying permission, possibility, or obligation.

EXAMPLE

- I do my homework. -> I ***must do*** my homework. (intensity)
- John sleeps with his cat. -> John ***is sleeping*** with his cat. (tense)
- John's classmates love him. -> John ***is loved*** by his classmates. (active to passive)
- You go to the restroom -> You ***may go*** to the restroom. (permission)

LESSON 5

Progressive (continuous) verbs must be used with appropriate forms of the verb "be" to function as verbs.

EXAMPLE

- The flowers ***are blooming*** in the garden. (O)
- The teacher ***is grading*** papers after class. (O)
- The teacher ***grading*** papers after class. (X)

EXPLANATION Without the helping verb "is," "grading" cannot function as the verb.

LESSON 6

Linking verbs are types of verbs that don't express action. Instead, they connect the subject of the verb to additional information about the subject. In other words, they link the subject to the rest of the sentence.

EXAMPLE

"Be" verbs	am, is, are, was, were, be, being, been • Alice is a doctor.
Sense perception verbs	look, taste, smell, sound, feel • The soup tastes delicious.
Other linking verbs	become, seem, appear, remain, turn, grow • John became a successful entrepreneur.

However, context is key as these verbs can also be action verbs or helping verbs in different sentences.

- Sheila tasted the apple.
- Alice is studying to become a doctor.

The first example uses "tasted" as an action verb, and the second example sentence uses "is" as a helping verb to the main verb "studying".

LESSON 7

Transitive verbs require a direct object to complete their meaning whereas intransitive verbs do not take a direct object.

EXAMPLE

Intransitive | Transitive | Both

- The time flies. (O)
- The time flies a person. (X)

Intransitive | **Transitive** | Both

- I like. (X)
- I like dogs. (O)

Intransitive | Transitive | **Both**

- The BTS sang in the car. (O)
- The BTS sang a song. (O)

EXPLANATION

To make it simple, read a subject and a verb, and if you wonder about what or whom, it is a transitive verb. Some verbs can be both transitive and intransitive.

VERB DRILL

Answers are provided on page 199~200.

INSTRUCTION

Underline the verbs in the following sentence, and mark **hv** for helping verbs, **av** for action verbs, and **lv** for linking verbs.

1

I should have practiced more to improve my skills and be better prepared for the challenge ahead.

2

The population of Amur tigers has been severely depleted due to habitat loss, poaching, and human encroachment.

3

The XYZ company is still deciding on the best course of action to take in response to the changing market conditions and evolving customer needs.

4

Malcolm X was a prominent civil rights leader and activist in the United States during the mid-20th century.

5

Thomas Paines speech sounded eloquent, impactful, and resonant with powerful rhetoric.

6

The apple that the witch gave to Snow White tasted sweet, but it was laced with a deadly poison.

CONJUNCTIONS

WHAT IS A CONJUNCTION

A conjunction is a part of speech that connects words, phrases, or clauses within a sentence. There are three main types of conjunctions: coordinating, correlative, and subordinating conjunctions.

<table>
<tr><th colspan="2">Type</th><th>List</th><th>Role</th></tr>
<tr><td colspan="2">Coordinating</td><td>and but or so yet
for nor</td><td>Connects words, phrases, and clauses</td></tr>
<tr><td colspan="2">Correlative</td><td>• both A and B
• either A or B
• neither A nor B
• not A but B
• not only A but(also) B</td><td>Paired words that act as one conjunction</td></tr>
<tr><td rowspan="4">Subordinate</td><td>Noun</td><td>that what why when
who if whether</td><td>Lead a noun clause</td></tr>
<tr><td>Adverbial</td><td>when before after
until while
although even though
even if so that
because since</td><td rowspan="2">Lead an adverbial clause – expressing time, condition, reason, purpose, or etc.</td></tr>
<tr><td>Adverbial (relative adverbial)</td><td>preposition + which/whom</td></tr>
<tr><td>Adjective (relative pronoun)</td><td>that who whom
which whose</td><td>Lead an adjective clause (relative pronoun clause)</td></tr>
</table>

LESSON 1 **Coordinating conjunctions connect words, phrases, and clauses that are equally important in the context.**

EXAMPLE

- a car ***or*** bike
- for the people ***and*** by the people
- I like to study ***but*** my mom doesn't let me. (X)
- I like to study, ***but*** my mom doesn't let me. (O)

EXPLANATION A comma is needed when two clauses are joined by a coordinating conjunction.

LESSON 2 **Correlative Conjunctions are used in pairs.**

EXAMPLE

- Many people exercise ***not only*** to stay fit ***<u>and also</u>*** to sleep well at night. (X)
- Many people exercise ***not only*** to stay fit ***<u>but also</u>*** to sleep well at night. (O)

EXPLANATION Not only should be partnered with but also.

LESSON 3 **Conjunctions that make a whole clause a noun:**

That	What	Why	When	Who	Whether	If

EXAMPLE

1. [That James has many friends] ***make*** me happy. (X)
   [That James has many friends] ***makes*** me happy. (O)
2. Only God knows [when ***will Jesus*** come again]. (X)
   Only God knows [when ***Jesus will*** come again]. (O)
3. Scientists found out [the fastest sperm is not necessarily the one that fertilizes the egg]. (O)

EXPLANATION

1. When a noun clause is used as a subject, it is a singular count.
2. When an interrogative conjunction is used to form a noun clause, the verb should follow the subject.
3. The conjunction that can be omitted when used as an object of a sentence.

LESSON 4 **Adverbial clause can come before or after the independent clause.**

EXAMPLE

- ***Because Copernicus believed Earth orbits the sun,*** Copernicus's model of the universe differs from Ptolemy's

- Copernicus's model of the universe differs from Ptolemy's ***because Copernicus believed Earth orbits the sun.***

EXPLANATION **General rule** is that if an adverbial clause comes first, a comma is needed at the end of it. But when it comes to the latter part of the sentence, a comma is not needed.

LESSON 5 **The conjunction *while* does not follow the general rule.**

EXAMPLE

- John cleans the bedroom, ***while his wife prepares breakfast.*** (X)
- John cleans the bedroom ***while his wife prepares breakfast.*** (O)
- ***While his wife prepares breakfast,*** John cleans the bedroom (O)

- John likes to play computer games ***while his wife likes to go shopping.*** (X)
- John likes to play computer games, ***while his wife likes to go shopping.*** (O)
- ***While his wife likes to go shopping,*** John likes to play computer games. (O)

EXPLANATION If ***while*** is used to convey simultaneous actions, then a <u>comma is not needed</u>. However, if ***while*** is used to compare two thoughts, a <u>comma is needed.</u>

LESSON 6

Adverbial conjunctions and conjunctive adverbs are different. Adverbial conjunctions are literally "conjunctions" whereas conjunctive adverbs are "adverbs", not conjunctions. That is to say, conjunctive adverbs cannot physically join two clauses, they only connect the ideas. The examples are *however, therefore, also, hence, and moreover.*

EXAMPLE

- Mike likes to study, ***but*** he often finds it difficult to concentrate for long periods of time. (O)
- Mike likes to study, ***however*** he often finds it difficult to concentrate for long periods of time. (X)
- Mike likes to study, ***however,*** he often finds it difficult to concentrate for long periods of time. (X)
- Mike likes to study; ***however,*** he often finds it difficult to concentrate for long periods of time. (O)
- Mike likes to study. ***However,*** he often finds it difficult to concentrate for long periods of time. (O)

EXPLANATION You can join two clauses by adding a semicolon or separate them by adding a period.

NOTE BOX

- **Conjunctions are essential for forming complex and compound sentences, adding variety and depth to writing.**
- **Proper use of conjunctions and punctuation ensures clarity and coherence in communication.**
- **Be mindful of the rules governing different conjunctions to avoid common grammatical errors.**

CONJUNCTION DRILL

Answers are provided on page 200.

INSTRUCTION

<u>Underline</u> the conjunctions in the following sentence. Mark CC for coordinating, CO for correlative, NC for noun, ADVC for adverbial, and ADJC for adjective conjunctions. As for the coordinating and correlative conjunctions, put parenthesis around the words they join.

1

The politician emphasized in her speech that her policies would not only benefit the economy but also prioritize social justice and environmental protection.

2

The university's mission statement highlights its commitment not only to academic excellence but also to diversity and inclusion among its student body and faculty.

3

The hotel's website promotes its dedication not only to luxurious amenities and comfort but also to sustainability and eco-friendliness.

4

Sarah, who cried all night long, finally fell asleep in the early hours of the morning and woke up feeling exhausted and emotionally drained.

5

The book, which was written by a famous author, has received rave reviews from critics around the world because it tackles important social issues and offers a fresh perspective on the human condition.

6

While Jake was in the bathroom, his phone rang incessantly, and he missed several important calls from his boss.

7

Sarah received a gift that her boyfriend prepared for Valentine's Day and loved it.

8

Sarah received a gift that her boyfriend prepared for Valentine's Day and was excited to give as a token of his love and appreciation.

9

That Vicky got a perfect score on the SAT made her parents extremely proud of her.

INTERJECTION

WHAT IS INTERJECTION

Interjections are words or phrases that are used to express emotions, feelings, or attitudes.

LESSON 1 Typically used in isolation or at the beginning of a sentence

- "wow"
- "oops"
- "ah"
- "oh"
- "hurray"
- "alas"
- "ouch"
- "hey"
- "um"
- "well"

*** **NOTE** *** **Interjections are not tested on the SAT.**

2

VERB IN-DEPTH

- ❑ VERB TENSE
- ❑ VERB VOICE

VERB TENSE

WHAT IS VERB TENSE

Verb tense refers to the different forms that a verb can take to indicate the time period in which an action occurs or the state of being.

12 VERB TENSES

	Past	**Present**	**Future**
Simple	I taught English.	I teach English.	I will teach English.
Progressive	I was teaching English.	I am teaching English.	I will be teaching English.
Perfect	I had taught English.	I have taught English.	I will have taught English.
Perfect Progressive	I had been teaching English.	I have been teaching English.	I will have been teaching English.

SIMPLE TENSES

	Past	Present	Future
Simple	I taught English.	I teach English.	I will teach English.

LESSON 1

<u>The simple present tense</u> is a verb form used to describe actions, habits, general truths, and states of being that are ongoing or repeated in the present. It is used to talk about facts, routines, schedules, and things that are generally true.

EXAMPLE 1 **The simple present tense is used to express the condition of the present point**

- Although she did not sleep last night, she *feels* good.

EXAMPLE 2 **The simple present tense is used to express the unchangeable truth and general facts**

- The sun *rises* in the east.

EXAMPLE 3 **The simple present tense is used to express jobs and repeated actions**

- Hulk *goes* to the gym every day after work.

EXAMPLE 4 **The simple present tense is used to express fixed schedule that is happening in the future**

- The plane *leaves* for London at eight tomorrow morning.

EXAMPLE 5 **The simple present tense is used to express a precondition**

- We will start the meeting as soon as he *arrives*.

LESSON 2 **The simple past tense is an action that happened and finished in the past.**

EXAMPLE

- New technology ***allowed*** scientists to investigate cell-based therapies to treat diseases.

LESSON 3 **The simple future tense is an action that will happen in the future.**

EXAMPLE

- Gatsby desperately believes that money is omnipotent and ***will allow*** him to marry his true love, Daisy.

PROGRESSIVE TENSES "be+Ving"

	Past	Present	Future
Progressive	I was teaching English.	I am teaching English.	I will be teaching English.

LESSON 1 **The present progressive tense shows an action that is happening in the present or in near future.**

EXAMPLE

- Do not turn the TV off. I ***am watching*** it.
- John ***is leaving*** next week.

LESSON 2 **The past progressive tense shows an ongoing action what was happening in the past.**

EXAMPLE

- My mother called me when I ***was playing*** a computer game.

LESSON 3 **The future progressive tense shows an action that is scheduled to happen.**

EXAMPLE

- Michelle ***will be conducting*** a workshop for her employees on the intuition of new safety procedures.

LESSON 4

Special features of progressive tenses:

Progressive tenses have two characteristics- temporary action and incomplete action. Therefore, you cannot use progressive tenses to show completion or generality.

Below are the state verbs that cannot be used as progressive tenses.

Be Verbs	be	seem	appear			
Possessive Verbs	have	own	possess			
Emotion Verbs	like	love	feel	smell	hate	dislike
Cognition Verbs	know	believe	think	imagine	agree	
Etc.	equal	contain	resemble			

EXAMPLE

- John ***is knowing*** you. (X)
- John ***knows*** you. (O)
- I ***am having*** a pen. (X) ➡ have = own
- I ***am having*** breakfast. (O) ➡ have = eat
- Jennifer ***is being*** nice. (Jennifer is normally not nice. Nice is a temporal behavior.)
- Jennifer ***is*** nice. (She was nice, she is nice, and maybe she will be nice.)

EXPLANATION

Verbs that describe states, conditions, and mental or emotional processes are often not used in the progressive tense because they do not typically indicate an ongoing action. In other words, the verbs that cannot be stopped when intended **CANNOT** be used in the progressive tense. The word "being" in SAT is often wrong for the above reason. For example, it is wrong to say "The car is being spacious."

PERFECT TENSES

	Past	Present	Future
Perfect	I had taught English.	I have taught English.	I will have taught English.

LESSON 1

The present perfect tense is a verb form that refers to events that have occurred at unspecified times before the present moment. It's used to show an action that happened at an indefinite time in the past, or when the action started in the past and continues into the present.

EXAMPLE 1 **The present perfect tense conveys continuous action. It is used mostly with the following words: since, for, always, up to now, and so far.**

- Alex *has gone* to Korea for 5 years.

EXPLANATION Alex went to Korea and is still in Korea.

EXAMPLE 2 **The present perfect tense conveys the past experience, and it is used mostly with one of the following adverbs: ever, never, lately, recently, and before.**

- Alex *has been to Korea* and is now sharing his knowledge and experiences with his friends and family.

EXPLANATION Alex had an experience of visiting Korea.

EXAMPLE 3 **The present perfect tense conveys the result that affects or implies the present condition.**

- Alex *has deleted* all her emails.

EXPLANATION Alex deleted all her emails so now she no longer has any emails.

EXAMPLE 4 **The present perfect tense conveys an action that has happened or been completed just now. It is used mostly with one of the following adverbs: just, already, and yet.**

- Alex *has just finished* her homework.

EXPLANATION Alex finished her homework a moment ago.

LESSON 2 **List of words that should not be used with the present perfect tense.**

Last (winter) yesterday in (1920) (a month) ago

EXAMPLE

- I have used my smart phone in 2010. (X)
- I have used my smart phone since 2010. (O)

EXPLANATION Since the present perfect tense signifies the present, adverbs that express only the past cannot be used with it.

LESSON 3 **The Past Perfect Tense shows a past action that occurred prior to another past action.**

EXAMPLE

- By the time I arrived at the party, everyone ***had*** already ***left***.
- They ***had been married*** for ten years before they decided to have children.

EXPLANATION When you spot the past perfect tense on the answer choice, look for the past tense or phrase that expresses the past. Without it, you cannot use the past perfect tense.

LESSON 4 **The Future Perfect Tense shows a future action that will occur prior to another future action.**

EXAMPLE

- By next year, I ***will have graduated*** from college.
- In ten years, she ***will have published*** five books.

NOTE BOX

The past and future perfect tenses go well with the preposition "by."

PERFECT PROGRESSIVE TENSES

It is a combination of perfect and progressive tenses.

	Past	Present	Future
Perfect Progressive	I had been teaching English.	I have been teaching English.	I will have been teaching English.

LESSON 1

The present perfect progressive shows a repeated action that has started from the past, continues to the present, and probably carries on in the future.

EXAMPLE

- I *have been using* my cell phone for two years.

LESSON 2

The past perfect progressive shows a continuous past action that occurred prior to another past time.

EXAMPLE

- I *had been using* my cell phone for two years before I bought a new one.

LESSON 3

The future perfect progressive shows a future continuous action that will be completed prior to another future time.

EXAMPLE

- Next year, I *will have been using* my cellphone for 2 years.

LESSON 4

When joined by a conjunction, verb tenses should logically be matched with the context.

EXAMPLE

In an effort to preserve the delicate balance of ecosystems, conservationist Emily Johnson has proposed the installation of underwater barriers along the coast to prevent the intrusion of invasive species into the sensitive marine habitats. These barriers would create a physical barrier and ______ advanced monitoring technology to detect and deter the entry of nonnative species, safeguarding the native biodiversity and maintaining the ecological integrity of the coastal ecosystems.

A) employs
B) employ
C) employing
D) employed

EXPLANATION

Besides the verb from the answer choices, what other verb does the conjunction connect? It's would create. It expresses a hypothetical or conditional action in the future. It indicates that if the proposed action (installation of underwater barriers) were to take place, the result or outcome mentioned in the sentence would be achieved.

Therefore, the tense for the answer should also be hypothetical, so it should be read "would create ~ and would employ." The redundant "would" can be omitted, and the answer is B.

Skill for solving the actual questions

SCENARIO 1 **The answer choices show not only various verb tenses but also singular and plural forms.**

EXAMPLE

Computer scientists Larry Page and Sergey Brin co-founded Google, the world's largest search engine, which _______ the way people access and share information online.

A) revolutionize
B) were revolutionizing
C) has revolutionized
D) have revolutionized

Step 1

It is more likely a subject and verb number agreement question. Always check it first. Also, when you see the answer choices, you can notice that only one is in a singular form.

Step 2

Check the subject for the verb. It is the "engine" – singular.

Step 3

Check the answer choices, and only C is singular. The answer is C.

SCENARIO 2 **The answer choices show various verb tenses without showing the singular and plural forms at the same time.**

EXAMPLE

The Venus flytrap (Dionaea muscipula) is a carnivorous plant that traps insects by using specialized leaves that snap shut when triggered by small hairs on their surface, and then _______ digestive enzymes to break down their prey.

A) had secreted
B) secreted
C) would secrete
D) secretes

Step 1

Try to look for words or phrases that give you a hint for choosing a verb tense. Since there is no adverb that tells the time, look for verbs.

Step 2

You can easily tell that this sentence deals with facts, using "is" as a main verb and "traps" and "snap" as verbs for the subordinating clauses.

Step 3

The answer is D. Quite obvious right?

Step 4

You could spot the conjunction "when," but be careful! The word "triggered" is not a verb expressing past tense. Since it is a participle that modifies "leaves," don't select the past tense (the answer choice B) to match with "triggered."

VERB TENSE PROBLEM SET

Answers are provided on page 201.

1

By the time we arrived at the restaurant, the chef had already prepared our meals. We were pleasantly surprised to find that our food ________ ready as soon as we sat down to eat.

Which choice completes the text so that it conforms to the conventions of Standard English?

A) was

B) is

C) has been

D) had been

2

I ________ my homework before my friends came over to visit. I was able to relax and spend time with them without worrying about my assignments.

Which choice completes the text so that it conforms to the conventions of Standard English?

A) will finish

B) am finishing

C) have finished

D) had finished

3

As long as people require accurate interpretations, real-life interpreters ________ essential.

Which choice completes the text so that it conforms to the conventions of Standard English?

A) remains

B) will remain

C) will have remained

D) had remained

4

Some books don't withstand the test of time, while others ________ relevant and influential for generations.

Which choice completes the text so that it conforms to the conventions of Standard English?

A) had remained

B) remain

C) remained

D) could have remained

5

The researchers ________ unable to pinpoint the exact source of the outbreak, nor could they determine the specific steps necessary to prevent future outbreaks.

Which choice completes the text so that it conforms to the conventions of Standard English?

A) are

B) were

C) had been

D) will have been

6

Salespeople drive hundreds of miles every week. Their cars' make and model ________ often the envy of their peers.

Which choice completes the text so that it conforms to the conventions of Standard English?

A) were

B) are

C) had been

D) will have been

7

Whenever Maria played the piano, the melody ________ the entire room.

Which choice completes the text so that it conforms to the conventions of Standard English?

A) will fill

B) fills

C) would fill

D) had filled

8

As per Johnson, a reputable weather forecaster, tropical storms in the Atlantic during 2019 generated high amounts of rainfall, some of which overflowed into neighboring states and ________ severe flooding.

Which choice completes the text so that it conforms to the conventions of Standard English?

A) causes

B) will cause

C) caused

D) had caused

9

For instance, on the Law School Admission Test (LSAT), students aspiring to study intellectual property law ________ higher than students in all but five other specializations.

Which choice completes the text so that it conforms to the conventions of Standard English?

A) has scored

B) have scored

C) scores

D) to score

10

Every time Sarah rode her bicycle, the wind ________ through her hair.

Which choice completes the text so that it conforms to the conventions of Standard English?

A) whistles

B) has whistled

C) had whistled

D) would whistle

11

At the age of 15, I decided that I ________ and I have honored that commitment to myself for the past 30 years.

Which choice completes the text so that it conforms to the conventions of Standard English?

A) will never smoke

B) will never be smoking

C) would never smoke

D) would have never smoked

12

For the last fifteen years, the SAT test ________ a significant factor in determining college admission in the United States.

Which choice completes the text so that it conforms to the conventions of Standard English?

A) is

B) has been

C) had been

D) is being

13

The fossil records indicate that the flora of the Carboniferous period of prehistory ________ approximately 300 to 350 million years ago.

Which choice completes the text so that it conforms to the conventions of Standard English?

A) has flourished

B) flourished

C) had flourished

D) flourishes

14

The storm ________ by the time we woke up in the morning. We were relieved to see that there was no damage and we could continue with our day as planned.

Which choice completes the text so that it conforms to the conventions of Standard English?

A) passed

B) was passing

C) had passed

D) would pass

VERB VOICE

WHAT IS VERB VOICE

The voice of a verb refers to the relationship between the action or state described by the verb and the subjects and objects of the sentence.
There are two voices in English: active voice and passive voice.

Active	The subject of a sentence does the action.
Passive	The subject of a sentence receives the action.

LESSON 1

Only transitive verbs- the verbs that require objects- can be converted from active to passive. This is because the object of a sentence has to become a subject.

EXAMPLE

- Many love this book.
- This book is loved by many.

EXPLANATION

As you can see from the example sentences, more words are required to make a passive voice, but the sentence means the same. That is why the SAT generally prefers the active voice.

LESSON 2

The tense for the passive voice is decided by the "be" verb, not the verb that follows it.

EXAMPLE

- The floor ***is being*** swept. (present progressive tense)
- The ball ***was*** thrown by the legendary pitcher Byung Hyun. (past tense)
- The cake ***is*** baked by Mary. (present tense)

LESSON 3

Writing a sentence with a passive voice is not wrong, but it often becomes wordy. For this reason, we only use the passive voice when we have specific reasons: to focus on the action or the recipient of the action rather than the person or thing performing the action. This is often used when the doer of the action is unknown, unimportant, general, or should not be the focus of the sentence.

EXAMPLE

- Someone stole my bag.

  ➡ My bag is stolen.

- People say that the best things in life are free.

  ➡ It is said that the best things in life are free.

NOTE BOX

Neither an active nor passive voice is grammatically wrong, and the context of a sentence decides which is better. However, when it comes to solving the SAT, the active voice is most likely the answer.

Building skills to solve the actual questions

SCENARIO 1 **Sentence starts with a participial phrase(modifier).**

EXAMPLE Awarded the Nobel Prize in Physics in 1909, ________.

A) Italian inventor Guglielmo Marconi pioneered the development of long-distance wireless communication.

B) the development of long-distance wireless communication was pioneered by Italian inventor Guglielmo Marconi.

C) Italian inventor Guglielmo Marconi's development pioneered long-distance wireless communication.

D) Guglielmo Marconi, an Italian inventor, who pioneered the development of long-distance wireless communication.

Step 1

Since the participle is "awarded," the subject has to be the person who received the award. You can eliminate B and C because the development cannot be awarded the Nobel Prize.

Step 2

Find which answer choice has a grammatical error. D is a fragment. Therefore, the answer is A.

NOTE

It is not an active/passive voice question, but I just wanted to show you how the SAT test makers make the answer choice with passive voice wrong. Look at answer choice B. The context itself is the same as that of answer choice A. However, because the test makers inserted the modifier *Awarded the Nobel Prize in Physics in 1909*, at the beginning of the sentence, B cannot be the answer.

SCENARIO 2 **Sentence starts with a participial phrase(modifier), and you could only eliminate two answer choices.**

EXAMPLE

Filled with pictures and items of many great leaders of America, __________ showcased the life and legacy of the civil rights leader.

A) Kimberly exhibited Martin Luther King Jr.'s miniature room; it
B) recently Kimberly exhibited Martin Luther King Jr.'s miniature room which
C) Kimberly's recent exhibition of Martin Luther King Jr.'s miniature room
D) Martin Luther King Jr.'s miniature room was recently exhibited by Kimberly and

Step 1

Since the subject should be filled with pictures and items, you can eliminate A and B, whose subject is Kimberly.

Step 2

Now, you need to determine whether the exhibition or the room was filled with pictures and items. You can read the context and choose the answer. The answer is C.

Step 3

Again, it is not an active/passive voice question. However, sometimes it is not easy to grasp the context of the sentence, especially when it contains scientifical terms. In that case, look at the voice of the verb. The active voice will most likely be the answer.

VERB VOICE DRILL 1

Answers are provided on page 201.

INSTRUCTION **Change active to passive voice if possible.**

1. The janitor is sweeping the floor.

2. The airplane flies through the clouds.

3. Mariah sang a beautiful rendition of the classic ballad.

4. Architect Mike meticulously drafted the plans for the new building.

5. Gordon Ramsay's expert palate quickly identified the flaws in the dish.

VERB VOICE DRILL 2

Answers are provided on page 201.

INSTRUCTION

Underline the verbs in the following sentences and indicate whether the voice is active or passive.

1 All students will be given opportunities to express their thoughts on this matter.

2 The company has implemented several new policies and procedures to improve efficiency and ensure compliance with industry regulations.

3 For your convenience, a user-friendly interface has been designed with intuitive navigation and clear labeling to ensure ease of use for all users.

4 All requirement must be met in order for prospective students to be considered for admission into the program.

5 The Microhard has installed the new security system to protect their confidential data.

6 By joining the company's loyalty program, customers can earn points for their purchases and redeem them for exclusive rewards and discounts.

3

SENTENCE STRUCTURE

❑ PHRASE vs. CLAUSE

PHRASE vs. CLAUSE

LESSON 1 **Phrase is a group of words that act as one part of speech**

EXAMPLE

Prepositional phrase	during the meeting
Verb phrase	will have studied
Noun phrase	becoming a doctor

EXPLANATION Prepositional phrases can be either adjective or adverb phrases, depending on how it is used in the sentence.

LESSON 2 **Clause is a group of words arranged as a sentence structure. In other words, it contains (a subject) + a verb + (a modifier). A Subject or a modifier can sometimes be omitted, but a verb must be present.**

EXAMPLE

- I slept late at night
- the architecture is beautiful
- one of her friends gave Shelia a warm embrace

EXPLANATION If the first letter is capitalized and a period is added at the end, those clauses become sentences.

LESSON 3 **There are two types of clauses: an independent and a subordinate clause.**

EXAMPLE

- Because you are studying with this book, (subord.) you will excel on the SAT (indep.).

EXPLANATION Independent clause is a group of words that can stand alone as a sentence. It often conveys more importance than the subordinate clause. Subordinate(dependent) clause is a group of words that must be used with an independent clause or as a part of an independent clause.

LESSON 4

A type of conjunction decides whether a clause is independent or subordinate when there is more than one clause.

EXAMPLE

- ***My mom saw my recent SAT score report***, but ***I did not notice it.*** – two independent clauses
- ***That I love this book*** is a fact. – A subject in a sentence.
- ***As it grew dark***, people became scared. – An adverbial clause that expresses the time.
- This is the book ***which I was looking for***. – Adjective(relative pronoun) clause that modifies the noun 'book'.

EXPLANATION

You do not need to discern the types of clauses used in a sentence, but you need to know where a clause starts and ends so that you can see how many clauses are in a sentence and whether the sentence needs a conjunction or not.

4

VERBID

- GERUND
- INFINITIVE
- PARTICIPLE

GERUND

WHAT IS GERUND

A gerund is a verb form that ends in -ing and functions as a noun.

Form	V+ing
Role	Noun

LESSON 1 Gerund phrases as subjects

EXAMPLE

- Making friends have become easier thanks to SNS. (X)
- Making friends has become easier thanks to SNS. (O)

EXPLANATION The gerund phrase ***Making friends*** is the subject of the sentence. Since it is singular, it takes a singular verb (***has***).

LESSON 2 Verbs that take gerunds as objects

EXAMPLE

- The subcommittee is considering ***to postpone*** the proposed legislation. (X)
- The subcommittee is considering ***postponing*** the proposed legislation. (O)

LESSON 3 Gerunds as objects of prepositions

EXAMPLE

- I am responsible ***for set up*** a new museum exhibition. (X)
- I am responsible ***for setting*** up a new museum exhibition. (O)

NOTE BOX

While this specific grammar point may not appear on the SAT, knowing common verb patterns can enhance your writing.

INFINITIVE

WHAT IS INFINITIVE

An infinitive is the base form of a verb, usually preceded by to. Infinitives can function as nouns, adjectives, or adverbs.

Form	To + Verb Root
Role	Noun, adjective, or adverb

LESSON 1 Infinitives as nouns

EXAMPLE

- *To drink water in the morning* is strongly recommended.

EXPLANATION The infinitive phrase ***To drink water*** acts as the subject of the sentence.

LESSON 2 Infinitives as adjectives

EXAMPLE

- My plan ***to lose weight*** has failed.

EXPLANATION The infinitive phrase ***to lose weight*** modifies the noun ***plan***.

LESSON 3 Infinitives as adverbs

EXAMPLE

- I went to Korea *to learn Korean.*

EXPLANATION The infinitive phrase ***to learn Korean*** explains ***why*** I went to Korea; it shows purpose.

LESSON 4 Do not confuse the infinitive "to" with the preposition "to."

EXAMPLE

- John devoted himself ***to write*** songs. (X)
- John devoted himself ***to writing*** songs. (O)
- Michael is looking forward ***to see*** you again. (X)
- Michael is looking forward ***to seeing*** you again. (O)
- Infuriated citizens objected ***to pay*** taxes. (X)
- Infuriated citizens objected ***to paying*** taxes. (O)

EXPLANATION Some verbs or expressions are followed by the preposition to, and when to is a preposition, it must be followed by a gerund (-ing form), not an infinitive.

Some words that take the Preposition "to"	
Be used to –ing (as in accustomed to)	devote (oneself) to –ing
Look forward to –ing	object to –ing
Prefer A (–ing) to B (–ing)	take to –ing (as in being obsessed)

LESSON 5 Infinitives do not act as verbs.

EXAMPLE

- Scientists ***to believe*** that the main cause of the increase in the earth's temperature is carbon dioxide. (X)

EXPLANATION *To believe* is an infinitive and cannot serve as the main verb. The sentence requires a conjugated verb (***believe***).

Scientists ***believe*** that the main cause of the increase in the earth's temperature is carbon dioxide. (O)

PARTICIPLE

WHAT IS PARTICIPLE

Participle is a verb-like form that acts as an adjective.

Form	ACTIVE VOICE V+ing PASSIVE VOICE V+ed(p.p.)
Role	Adjective
Example	My ***shaving*** device is an expensive one. Those ***planted*** trees look nice

LESSON 1 Participles modifying nouns following them

EXAMPLE

- ***Pollinated*** flowers should develop into fruits.

EXPLANATION The past participle ***pollinated*** modifies ***flowers***, describing which flowers.

LESSON 2 Participles modifying nouns before them

EXAMPLE

- Flowers ***pollinated by bees*** develop into fruits.

EXPLANATION The participial phrase ***pollinated by bees*** modifies ***flowers***. Note that ***pollinated*** is not acting as a verb here; there is no auxiliary verb (**be** verb) before it.

LESSON 3

When two clauses have the same subject, you can combine them by turning one clause into a participial phrase. Then add a comma accordingly.

EXAMPLE

- The store opens at 9 A.M. The store closes at 10 P.M.
  - ➡ Opening at 9 A.M., the store closes at 10 P.M.
  - ➡ The store opens at 9 A.M., closing at 10 P.M.

- John walked out of the room. He slammed the door behind him.
  - ➡ John walked out of the room, slamming the door behind him.

EXPLANATION

Because the comma is after or before the participial phrase, you know the subject of the sentence is doing the action of the participle.

To put it simply, a participial phrase should modify the subject of the sentence, especially when it is the beginning of a sentence.

If the comma before the word slamming is omitted, then ***slamming*** no longer modifies the subject; instead, it modifies the ***room*** – which makes no sense.

LESSON 4

Participial phrases at the end of a sentence can sometimes modify the object of the verb or the entire preceding clause.
Participial phrases can be formed by transforming clauses, allowing for more concise and fluid sentences. Here is a step-by-step process to convert two sentences into one sentence with a participial phrase.

EXAMPLE

- The research center has secured funding. This allows it to begin the preliminary research.
  - ➡ The research center has secured funding, ***and this allows*** it to begin the preliminary research.
    - ➡ The research center has secured funding, ***which allows*** it to begin the preliminary research.
      - ➡ The research center has secured funding, ***allowing*** it to begin the preliminary research.
- Michelangelo wanted a painting to hang in the museum's grand hall, ***which would be surrounded*** by ornate golden frames that would draw visitors' attention.
  - ➡ Michelangelo wanted a painting to hang in the museum's grand hall, ***surrounded*** by ornate golden frames that would draw visitors' attention.

EXPLANATION Usually, when a comma is not present, a participial phrase modifies the word directly in front of it. When a comma precedes a participial phrase, the phrase modifies the subject. However, if a participial phrase modifies the object of a sentence and is separated from it by a modifier (such as a prepositional phrase), a comma is used.

See the last example: ***Surrounded*** modifies ***the painting,*** not ***Michelangelo***.

LESSON 5

Dangling participle – common mistakes people make!

EXAMPLE

- *Frustrated by the lack of progress,* the validity of the researchers' methods was questioned. (X)
- *Frustrated by the lack of progress,* the researchers questioned the validity of their methods. (O)

EXPLANATION A dangling participle is an adjective phrase that modifies the wrong noun in a sentence. In this case, since the participial phrase is at the beginning of the sentence, the subject should be ***frustrated***, and the ***validity*** cannot be ***frustrated***.

LESSON 6

A participle is not a verb. In other words, the progressive verb form alone cannot be a verb. It needs a "be" verb to make the progressive form act as a verb in a sentence.

EXAMPLE

- A boy ***running*** to school. (X)
- A boy ***is running*** to school. (O)
- A boy ***runs*** to school. (O)

EXPLANATION Do not pick the choice that has a participle when a verb is needed in the sentence.

LESSON 7 **A level of detail and specificity of the main subject of a sentence can be added by adding a subject to the participial phrase.**

EXAMPLE

- As the sun set over the horizon, the tired travelers gathered around the campfire, <u>each</u> ***sharing*** stories of their adventures.

EXPLANATION Often the ***sharing*** part is left blank on the SAT grammar section. Be cautious not to create a run-on sentence by incorrectly conjugating the verb (e.g., using ***shares*** instead of ***sharing***).

LESSON 8 **The omission of a conjunction between two participial phrases can happen when it creates a sense of immediacy and flow in the sentence.**

EXAMPLE

- Ken hurried through the bustling marketplace, *scanning* the stalls for fresh vegetables, *planning* to prepare a delicious meal for his family that evening.

EXPLANATION It implies that these actions are happening one after the other or in quick succession, which can add a sense of urgency or dynamic movement to the narrative.

The question on the SAT writing would look like this.

Ken hurried through the bustling marketplace, scanning the stalls for colorful, fresh ______ planning to prepare a delicious meal for his family that evening.

A) vegetables
B) vegetables,
C) vegetables;
D) vegetables:

➡ B) *vegetables*, is the answer.

The comma after "colorful" helps separate the two adjectives, and the comma after "vegetables" is used to set off the participial phrase "planning to prepare a delicious meal for his family that evening." This maintains the correct punctuation and structure of the sentence.

NOTE BOX

When taking the SAT, do not pick the choice that has a participle when a verb is needed in the sentence.

LESSON 9 **Participial phrases can include adverbial conjunctions to express clear relationships.**

EXAMPLE

- Although I was standing in front of Harvard University, I couldn't fully grasp the depth of its history.

  ➡ Although standing in front of Harvard University, I couldn't fully grasp the depth of its history.

EXPLANATION It can be said "Standing in front of Harvard University, I couldn't fully grasp the depth of its history." However, inserting ***although*** to the sentence makes readers have clear understanding of the context.

LESSON 10 **A participial phrase can express an action that precedes that of the main clause by adding "having" in front of the phrase.**

EXAMPLE

- Patrick had (**past**) too much alcohol. Patrick is walking (**present**) like a duck.

  ➡ Having had too much alcohol, Patrick is walking like a duck.

- The storm had swept (**past perfect**) the entire city, and the storm moved (**past**) toward the east.

  ➡ Having swept the entire city, the storm moved toward the east.

- The building had been destroyed (**past perfect**) by fire, and the building was restored (**past**) by a renowned architect.

  ➡ Having been destroyed by fire, the building was restored by a renowned architect.

  ➡ Destroyed by fire, the building was restored by a renowned architect.

EXPLANATION ***Having been*** is not necessary when passive voice is expressed.

** Lessons 9 & 10 will not be on the SAT but are useful for enhancing your writing.*

VERBID DRILL 1

Answers are provided on page 201.

INSTRUCTION **Underline verbs and participles in the following sentences and indicate Par for participle, or V for verb.**

1. The tree planted in the backyard grew tall and strong, providing shade and beauty to the surrounding area.

2. The new security system installed at the office building includes state-of-the-art surveillance cameras, motion sensors, and access control measures.

3. Easy-to-follow assembly instructions included in the product box made it simple and straightforward for the customer to assemble the product at home without the need for any additional tools or equipment.

4. The actress cast in Resident Evil impressed audiences and critics alike with her compelling portrayal of the iconic protagonist.

5. Gold fascinated people in California during the mid-19th century because it was believed to be a source of immense wealth and opportunity.

VERBID DRILL 2

Answers are provided on page 201.

INSTRUCTION **Underline verbids or verbid phrases in the following sentences and indicate Ger for a gerund, Inf for an infinitive, or Par for a participial phrase.**

1 With the increasing use of technology among children, many parents are turning to software that allows them to monitor their kids' online activities and set restrictions on screen time.

2 John Muir, a renowned conservationist, dedicated his life to protecting and preserving natural landscapes.

3 While having dinner at a fancy restaurant, the couple enjoyed a delicious meal of prime rib and lobster, accompanied by a bottle of fine wine and a decadent dessert.

4 Many juries objected to the prosecution's evidence, citing a lack of credibility and insufficient proof to support the charges.

5 Having diverse facial expressions, Kimberly was able to effectively convey her emotions and thoughts during her presentation.

6 Understanding Albert Einstein's theory of relativity is crucial for grasping the fundamental nature of space, time, and gravity, and for unlocking new insights into the workings of the universe.

Answers are provided on page 203.

1

Despite its potential as a renewable energy source, harnessing solar power on a large scale poses significant challenges. Engineers and scientists are continually working on innovative solutions _____ these challenges and maximizing the efficiency of solar energy systems.

Which choice completes the text so that it conforms to the conventions of Standard English?

A) addressing

B) to address

C) addressed

D) having addressed

2

Inspired by the remarkable findings of Dr. Sarah Roberts, a team of scientists, led by Dr. Michael Anderson and Dr. Olivia Foster—renowned for their expertise—dedicated their efforts to unravel the mysteries of a rare genetic disorder. Through their extensive research, they aimed _____ a breakthrough treatment that has the potential to cure the condition.

Which choice completes the text so that it conforms to the conventions of Standard English?

A) discover

B) discovering

C) discovered

D) to discover

3

Motivated by a profound realization, the renowned author Jane Thompson embarked on a transformative journey of self-reflection and growth. Through her introspection, she learned the importance of _____ past mistakes and embracing personal growth.

Which choice completes the text so that it conforms to the conventions of Standard English?

A) repenting

B) to repent

C) repented

D) repent

4

Driven by their passion for environmental conservation, a group of dedicated volunteers, led by Mark Johnson and Emily Parker, worked tirelessly to raise awareness about sustainable practices. Their goal was _____ widespread support and participation in eco-friendly initiatives.

Which choice completes the text so that it conforms to the conventions of Standard English?

A) to garner

B) garnering

C) garnered

D) garner

5

Despite the abundance of resources in the area, the local community struggles with high unemployment rates. A research team conducted a comprehensive study ______ the root causes and potential solutions for this persistent issue.

Which choice completes the text so that it conforms to the conventions of Standard English?

A) uncovering

B) to uncover

C) uncovered

D) having uncovered

6

John Muir, a renowned conservationist, dedicated his life to protecting and preserving natural ______ in the hearts of many, Muir's passion for nature continues to inspire environmentalists worldwide.

Which choice completes the text so that it conforms to the conventions of Standard English?

A) landscapes to plant

B) landscapes, planted

C) landscapes. Planted

D) landscapes plant

7

Despite being surrounded by a bustling city, the park provides a peaceful retreat for visitors. Landscape architects and urban planners have carefully designed the park ______ a serene and harmonious environment.

Which choice completes the text so that it conforms to the conventions of Standard English?

A) creating

B) to create

C) created

D) having created

8

The challenging weather conditions did not deter the mountaineering team, who persevered and successfully reached the summit of the treacherous peak. Their determination and skill allowed them ______ an incredible feat of human achievement.

Which choice completes the text so that it conforms to the conventions of Standard English?

A) to accomplish

B) accomplishing

C) accomplished

D) accomplish

9

The vibrant fireworks display illuminated the night sky, captivating spectators with its colorful _____ a symphony of light and sound, the fireworks created a mesmerizing spectacle for all to enjoy.

Which choice completes the text so that it conforms to the conventions of Standard English?

A) bursts, emitting

B) bursts, to emit

C) bursts. Emitting

D) bursts have been emitting

10

When faced with a natural disaster, the community came together in unity to support those affected. Volunteers and organizations mobilized their efforts, _____ relief supplies and providing assistance to those in need.

Which choice completes the text so that it conforms to the conventions of Standard English?

A) deliver

B) to deliver

C) delivered

D) delivering

11

The city, despite its turbulent history, has undergone a remarkable transformation and emerged as a vibrant cultural hub. Artists and architects have contributed to _____ a unique urban landscape that celebrates the city's rich heritage.

Which choice completes the text so that it conforms to the conventions of Standard English?

A) creating

B) create

C) created

D) creation

12

The small rural community, though geographically isolated, has nurtured a strong sense of solidarity. Residents actively participate in _____ a close-knit community where support and cooperation are valued.

Which choice completes the text so that it conforms to the conventions of Standard English?

A) buildings

B) build

C) built

D) building

5

MODIFIER

- ❑ APPOSITIVE
- ❑ RELATIVE CONJUNCTION
- ❑ RESTRICTIVE vs. NONRESTRICTIVE

APPOSITIVE

WHAT IS APPOSITIVE

An appositive is a noun or noun phrase that renames or defines another noun right beside it.

LESSON 1

An appositive can be nonrestrictive (nonessential) or restrictive (essential). A nonrestrictive appositive adds extra information and is set off by commas, whereas a restrictive appositive is essential to the meaning of the sentence and is not set off by commas.

EXAMPLE

- ***A member of the BTS,*** Jimin Park is renowned for stunning dance moves. (nonrestrictive)
- The Viking helmet has become a popular symbol of Scandinavian heritage, ***a romanticized emblem of ancient warrior culture.*** (nonrestrictive)
- Buchi Emecheta, ***a Nigerian author,*** wrote many novels that deal with gender imbalance. (nonrestrictive)
- My friend ***Sarah*** is visiting next week. (restrictive)
  (If you have multiple friends, ***Sarah*** specifies which friend is visiting.)
- The novel ***1984*** depicts a dystopian future. (restrictive)
  (Specifies which novel is being discussed.)

EXPLANATION

On the SAT, you might not often encounter questions involving an appositive at the beginning of a sentence like in the first example, but understanding comma usage with appositives is crucial.

LESSON 2

When a noun or adjective is defined using another word, the conjunction "or" can be used to indicate that the word is an appositive.

EXAMPLE

- Mandatory, ***or compulsory*** volunteering is an oxymoron. (X)
- Mandatory, ***or compulsory,*** volunteering is an oxymoron. (O)

- When the Lotte World Tower was opened to the public in April 2017, it boasted the highest height of any building in Korea: 555 meters **or 1821 feet.** (X)
- When the Lotte World Tower was opened to the public in April 2017, it boasted the highest height of any building in Korea: 555 meters**, or 1821 feet.** (O)

EXPLANATION On the SAT, comma and boundary questions usually deal with appositives.

PARTICIPLE & APPOSITIVE DRILL

Answers are provided on page 198.

INSTRUCTION

Some of the complicated writing questions contain both the participial and appositive phrase to confuse the test takers. Underline and Mark P for participle and A for appositive so that you can choose the right answer.

1 The Deep Sea Research Institute has secured one of the largest government funding, allowing it to begin the preliminary research.

2 ACV corporation implemented a new policy, a four-day workweek, hoping to boost employee morale.

3 Samsung has recently released a new product line, a high-performance laptop, expanding its market reach.

4 Yuna Kim broke the world record, a feat that had never been accomplished before, inspiring a new generation of competitors.

5 Galileo Galilei is perhaps best known for inventing an early microscope and observing planets and stars, but he also dedicated himself to physics, the study of motion and force, demonstrating that the speed of fall of a heavy object is not proportional to its weight.

RELATIVE CONJUNCTIONS

Two sentences are relatives, meaning that they have some word in common. Making one of them a modifying clause, you need a "relative conjunction."

Type	List
Relative pronoun conjunctions	that / who / whom / which / whose
Relative adverbial conjunctions	preposition + which or whom /where / when / why

Antecedent	Subjective	Possessive	Objective
person	who	whose	who(m)
object, animal	which	whose	which
person, object, animal	that		that
already included	what (the thing which)		what (the thing which)

LESSON 1

When two clauses share a common noun, you can combine them using a relative pronoun to form a relative clause.

EXAMPLE

- Visitors can obtain a visitor's pass at the security office,
  and it(the security office) is located on the first floor.
  - ➡ Visitors can obtain a visitor's pass at the security office, ***which it*** is located on the first floor. (X)
  - ➡ Visitors can obtain a visitor's pass at the security office, ***which*** is located on the first floor. (O)

EXPLANATION

The basic concept is that a ***conjunction*** and a ***pronoun*** combine to form a relative conjunction.

EXAMPLE 2

- I have bought several bottles of expensive liquor, ***and*** some of ***them*** are gifts for my friends and family.

  ➡ I have bought several bottles of expensive liquor, some of ***which*** are gifts for my friends and family.

EXPLANATION Relative pronouns can be objects of prepositions, allowing for more complex sentences. Some of which refers back to several bottles of expensive liquor, connecting the two ideas smoothly.

LESSON 2 ***Who*** **is used as a subject complement and** ***whom*** **is used as an object pronoun in a sentence.**

EXAMPLE

- I like Max. ~~**Max**~~ lives in NY. (Subjective Case)

  ➡ I like Max, ***whom*** lives in NY. (X)

  ➡ I like Max, ***who*** lives in NY. (O)

EXPLANATION When it is a subjective case (a subject is erased in the modifying clause), only ***who*** can be used.

EXAMPLE 2

- I like Max. Sheila adores ~~**Max**~~. (Objective Case)

  ➡ I like Max, ***who*** Sheila adores. (O)

  ➡ I like Max, ***whom*** Sheila adores. (O)

EXPLANATION 2 When it is an objective case(an object is erased), both ***who*** and ***whom*** can be used.

NOTE BOX

Because both *who* and *whom* can be used for an objective case, the SAT only tests you on the subjective case, using *whom* – which you need to change to *who*.

LESSON 3 **A relative pronoun clause can also become a participial phrase.**

EXAMPLE

- The research center has secured funding, ***and this allows*** it to begin the preliminary research.

  ➡ The research center has secured funding, ***which allows*** it to begin the preliminary research.

  ➡ The research center has secured funding, ***allowing*** it to begin the preliminary research.

EXPLANATION The relative pronoun conjunction who and which can be omitted and change the verb to an appropriate participial form.

LESSON 4 **Relative Clauses can often be simplified to participial phrases.**

EXAMPLE

- Emmanuelle Charpentier and Jennifer Doudna, who won the 2020 Nobel Prize in Chemistry, replicated and subsequently reengineered the "genetic scissors." ***These are found*** in a particular species of DNA-cleaving bacteria, and ***that created*** a tool that is transforming the field of genetic technology.

  ➡ Emmanuelle Charpentier and Jennifer Doudna, who won the 2020 Nobel Prize in Cemistry, replicated and subsequently reengineered the "genetic scissors" ***which are found*** in a particular species of DNA-cleaving bacteria, ***which created*** a tool that is transforming the field of genetic technology.

  ➡ Emmanuelle Charpentier and Jennifer Doudna, who won the 2020 Nobel Prize in Chemistry, replicated and subsequently reengineered the "genetic scissors" ***found*** in a particular species of DNA-cleaving bacteria, ***creating*** a tool that is transforming the field of genetic technology.

EXPLANATION Do you see how the sentence becomes more concise?
The relative clause ***which are found*** becomes the participial phrase ***found***, making the sentence more concise.
The participial phrase ***creating*** replaces ***which created***, streamlining the sentence.

LESSON 5

Relative adverbial conjunctions: where, when, why

EXAMPLE

- The restaurant was very busy. We ate ***there*** last night.
  ➡ The restaurant ***where*** we ate last night was very busy.

- The reason is still unknown. He didn't come to the party ***for a reason***.
  ➡ The reason ***why*** he didn't come to the party is still unknown.

- The time was unforgettable. We saw the shooting stars ***at the time***.
  ➡ The time ***when*** we saw the shooting stars was unforgettable.

EXPLANATION ***Where*** should refer to a place, ***when*** time, and ***why*** reason.

LESSON 6

A preposition and a relative conjunction (which or whom) should be used to be more specific and to modify something beyond a place, time, and reason.

EXAMPLE

- The restaurant was very busy. We ate ***at the restaurant*** last night.
  ➡ The restaurant ***at which*** we ate last night was very busy.

- The restaurant was very busy. We ordered the most expensive meal ***in the restaurant*** last night.
  ➡ The restaurant ***in which*** we ordered the most expensive meal last night was very busy.

- Scientists conducted an experiment. Newly-made vaccines were injected into three mice ***in the experiment***.
  ➡ Scientists conducted an experiment ***in which*** newly-made vaccines were injected into three mice. (O)
  ➡ Scientists conducted an experiment ***where*** newly-made vaccines were injected into three mice. (X)

EXPLANATION ***Experiment*** is not a place, so ***where*** is inappropriate.
Use preposition + which to refer to things that are not places.

Building skills to solve the actual questions

SCENARIO 1 **The answer choices are about relative conjunctions.**

EXAMPLE The new software includes a feature _______ users can easily share files with one another.

A) in which
B) whereby
C) of which
D) where

Step 1

Divide the sentence into two clauses.

The new software includes a feature / Users can easily share files with one another

Step 2

Replace *which* with the antecedent, and put it at the end of the clause it is followed by, including the preceding preposition.

A) Users can easily share files with one another ***in the feature.***
B) Users can easily share files with one another ***by the feature(whereby).***
C) Users can easily share files with one another ***of the feature.***
D) ***Feature*** *is not a place.*

Step 3

Whereby means by which or through which, indicating the method by which users can share files. The answer is B.

RELATIVE CONJUNCTION DRILL

Answers are provided on page 204.

INSTRUCTION **Choose the correct relative conjunction**

1 Food critics (who / whom) specialize in evaluating fine dining establishments often have a discerning palate and pay close attention to factors such as presentation, flavor, and texture.

2 The rate (at which/on which) technology is advancing is unprecedented, and it's difficult to predict where we will be in just a few years.

3 The school has a program (in which/whereby) students can participate in a variety of extracurricular activities, such as sports and music.

4 The company has gained a reputation for innovation in its industry due to the speed (at which/ of which) it is developing new products.

5 The majestic chandelier hung from the ceiling, casting a brilliant light (on which/by which) the entire room was illuminated in a warm and inviting glow.

6 The clear blue lake reflected the surrounding mountains, creating a picturesque scene with the water (where/in which) hikers could cool off after their long trek.

7 The package contained a handwritten letter (from which/ in which) the recipient derived great joy.

8 The new building boasts a rooftop terrace (on which / whereby) employees can relax and enjoy the view.

9 The company conducted a thorough market analysis (on which / for which) it based its strategic decisions.

10 The project required extensive research, (to which) the team dedicated countless hours.

RELATIVE CONJUNCTION PROBLEM SET

Answers are provided on page 204.

1

The historical artifacts excavated by archaeologists in Egypt provided valuable insights into ancient __________ to reconstruct the rich tapestry of Egyptian history.

Which choice completes the text so that it conforms to the conventions of Standard English?

A) civilization and using their findings

B) civilization and their findings were used by them

C) civilization, and they used their findings

D) civilizations, whose artifacts and cultural remnants were used

2

An acclaimed author, J.K. Rowling wrote a series of fantasy __________ that captivated readers and left them eagerly anticipating the release of the next book.

Which choice completes the text so that it conforms to the conventions of Standard English?

A) novels whose chapters ended with cliffhangers

B) novels, their chapters ended with cliffhangers

C) novels, which had chapters ending with cliffhangers

D) novels, each of these chapters had a cliffhanger endings

RESTRICTIVE (ESSENTIAL) vs. NONRESTRICTIVE (NONESSENTIAL)

LESSON 1

A restrictive clause (also called an essential or defining clause) provides essential information about the noun it modifies and is necessary to the meaning of the sentence. Without it, the sentence would not make sense. <u>Restrictive clauses are not set off by commas.</u>

A nonrestrictive clause (also called a nonessential or non-defining clause) provides additional, nonessential information about the noun it modifies. The sentence would still make sense if the clause were removed. <u>Nonrestrictive clauses are set off by commas.</u>

EXAMPLE

- I will be rich. I found a chest, which contains gold bars. (X)
- I will be rich. I found a chest which contains gold bars. (O)
- I will be rich. I found a chest that contains gold bars. (O)

EXPLANATION

The main point is that the speaker is confident about becoming rich. Without the information that says "contains gold bars," readers wouldn't know why the speaker feels this way. Since the clause is essential to the meaning of the sentence, no comma should be used.
Note: The conjunction ***that*** always introduces a restrictive clause and is not set off by commas.

LESSON 2

When general words precede specific words, the information is usually considered essential or restrictive. This is because the specific information provides necessary details that are essential to the meaning of the sentence.

EXAMPLE

- *Teacher, Max* is a great English grammar teacher. He always makes difficult concepts easy to understand. (X)
- *Teacher Max* is a great English grammar teacher. He always makes it easy to understand difficult concept.(O)

EXPLANATION

Teacher is a general word, and *Max* is a specific name. Thus, a comma is unnecessary. For this reason, we don't usually use a comma to separate the title and name.

EXAMPLE 2

- In my chemistry class, the teacher used vinegar and ***the chemical compound, sodium bicarbonate,*** to show us the similar effect of how a volcano erupts. (X)

- In my chemistry class, the teacher used vinegar and ***the chemical compound sodium bicarbonate*** to show us the similar effect of how a volcano erupts. (O)

EXPLANATION Again, ***chemical compound*** is a general term, and the appositive ***sodium bicarbonate*** is a specific name. Thus, removing the appositive makes the noun too vague.

LESSON 3

When specific words precede general words, the information is usually considered nonessential or nonrestrictive.

EXAMPLE

- *Max a great English grammar teacher* always makes difficult concepts easy to understand. (X)

- *Max, a great English grammar teacher,* always makes difficult concepts easy to understand. (O)

6

PUNCTUATION

- ❒ COMMA (,)
- ❒ SEMICOLON (;)
- ❒ EM-DASH (-)
- ❒ COLON (:)
- ❒ APOSTROPHES (')

COMMAS (,)

WHAT IS A COMMA

A comma (,) is a punctuation mark used to indicate a brief pause in a sentence. It is a versatile punctuation mark with various uses in writing.

LESSON 1 **Use a comma before coordinating conjunctions when they separate two independent clauses.**

EXAMPLE

- I went grocery shopping, ***and*** my brother went to school.

LESSON 2 **Use a comma after introductory adverbial clauses or phrases.**

EXAMPLE

- ***When I go to school***, I usually take the bus or ride my bike.
- I usually take the bus or ride my bike ***when I go to school***.
  (No comma needed here because the adverbial clause is at the end.)

LESSON 3 **Use commas to separate items in a list of three or more.**

EXAMPLE

- I need to take my sunscreen, swimsuit, and sunglasses for my vacation.

LESSON 4 **Use commas to set off nonrestrictive words, phrases, or clauses**

EXAMPLE

- I'm going to the concert tonight to see my favorite band, *BTS*.
- My best friend, ***who lives in New York***, is coming to visit me next month.
- My best friend, ***a talented musician***, is coming over to play some new songs for me tonight.
- The vestigial, ***or nonfunctional***, tail is a remnant of evolutionary history.

EXPLANATION You can use "*or*" to present options, but you can also use it to define a word using an alternative word by framing it with commas.

LESSON 5 **Use a comma after an introductory modifier.**

EXAMPLE

- *In order to be successful*, you must work hard. (Adverbial phrase)
- *In general*, people tend to feel happier when they spend time with loved ones and engage in activities that they enjoy. (Adverbial phrase)
- *Running down the street*, Sarah felt the wind in her hair. (Participial phrase)

LESSON 6 **Use commas to set off conjunctive adverbs or transitional phrases.**

EXAMPLE

- *In addition*, we need to buy some groceries before we leave.
- *Meanwhile*, the other team scored two more goals.
- I, *however*, still plan to go to the party tonight.
- *Nevertheless*, I am determined to finish this project on time.

LESSON 7 **Use commas when the sequence of the adjectives is interchangeable. The general rule in English is that adjectives are placed in a specific order based on their category. The following is the usual order: opinion, size, age, shape, color, origin, material, and purpose. If the two adjectives fall into the same category, their sequence is interchangeable with a comma.**

EXAMPLE 1

- A loud, piercing scream came from the top of the mountain. (O)
- A piercing, loud scream came from the top of the mountain. (O)

EXPLANATION Both *loud* and *piercing* fall into the same category: opinion.

EXAMPLE 2

- A beautiful wooden table is needed. (O)
- A wooden beautiful table is needed. (X)

EXPLANATION In this case, *beautiful* expresses the opinion, while *wooden* describes the material. So, it would be ***a beautiful wooden table.***

LESSON 8 **Don't use commas when quotation marks set apart a word to show irony, sarcasm, or skepticism (scare quotes).**

EXAMPLE

- I'm sure he's "working" hard at his new job.

EXPLANATION In this sentence, the quotation marks around ***working*** indicate that the speaker is skeptical about the person's work effort. No comma is needed.

LESSON 9 **Don't use a single comma between a subject and a verb in a sentence.**

EXAMPLE

- The dog, barks loudly. (X)
- The dog barks loudly. (O)
- The dog, however barks loudly. (X)
- The dog, however, barks loudly. (O)
- The dog, in my room barks loudly. (X)
- The dog in my room, barks loudly. (X)
- The dog in my room barks loudly. (O)

EXPLANATION The subject and verb form a single unit, and adding a comma between them would disrupt the sentence's grammatical structure.

LESSON 10 **Don't use a comma immediately after a preposition.**

EXAMPLE

- There is a dog in, my room. (X)

LESSON 11 **A comma cannot join two independent clauses without a coordinating conjunction.**

EXAMPLE

- I went grocery shopping, my brother went to school. (X)

EXPLANATION Don't just use a comma to join two clauses. You need a conjunction.

LESSON 12 **Don't use a comma before *that* clause.**

EXAMPLE

- I know ***that*** he is coming to the party.
- The fact ***that*** he is coming to the party, which I learned yesterday, is good news.

EXPLANATION Most of the time, it is unnecessary to use a comma before a that clause.

COMMA DRILL

Answers are provided on page 205.

INSTRUCTION

With the mark below, indicate the purpose of the commas used in the following sentences:

- To list □
- To separate two clauses Δ
- To set off modifier(appositives, introductory modifiers, the nonrestrictives) O

1

In her analysis of Jane Austen's novel *Pride and Prejudice*, literary scholar Emma Thompson highlights how the book depicts the social conventions and constraints of Regency-era England, a period defined by strict social hierarchies, limited choices for women, and societal expectations based on class and wealth.

2

The invention of the Post-it Note can be traced back to a 3M scientist named Spencer Silver, who created a low-tack, reusable adhesive in the late 1960s. However, it wasn't until several years later that a colleague named Art Fry realized the adhesive's potential as a bookmark.

3

The idea for the Dyson vacuum cleaner came to inventor James Dyson in the 1970s, when he became frustrated with the poor performance of his own vacuum. After years of experimentation and refinement, Dyson developed a unique cyclonic system that revolutionized the way we think about vacuuming.

4

The invention of the modern automobile can be attributed to several different inventors and innovators, including Karl Benz, Gottlieb Daimler, and Henry Ford. However, it wasn't until Ford's introduction of the assembly line in the early 1900s that cars became affordable and accessible to the average person.

5

Throughout history, people in many cultures have used herbal remedies to treat common ailments such as headaches, indigestion, and colds. While modern medicine has largely replaced the use of herbs in clinical settings, herbal remedies continue to be a popular choice for people seeking natural alternatives to pharmaceutical drugs.

SEMICOLONS (;)

WHAT IS SEMICOLON

A semicolon (;) is a punctuation mark that is used to connect two closely related independent clauses within a sentence.

LESSON 1 **Semicolons separate two independent clauses.**

EXAMPLE

- I went grocery shopping; my brother went to school.

LESSON 2 **Use semicolons to separate items in a complex list when the items themselves contain commas.**

EXAMPLE

- The suspects for the murder of the 42-year-old crime reporter were John, the teacher, Tony, the janitor, and Sheila, the principal of the school. (X)
- The suspects for the murder of the 42-year-old crime reporter were John, the teacher; Tony, the janitor; and Sheila, the principal of the school. (O)

EXPLANATION Without semicolons, the list becomes confusing due to the commas within each item.

LESSON 3 **Separate clauses in a list when the clauses contain commas.**

EXAMPLE 1

- Max bought a computer to play Overwatch, Sheila bought a computer to learn Korean through self-study, and John bought a computer to watch and manage his stocks. (O)

EXPLANATION Because the sentence does not have commas within the clauses, you can easily see where each clause ends. What if there is a comma within the sentence? Let's see the next example sentence.

EXAMPLE 2

- Max bought a computer to play Overwatch, a shooting game that requires a top-notch graphics card, Sheila bought a computer to learn Korean through self-study, and John bought a computer to watch and manage his stocks. (X)

EXPLANATION Adding a modifier with a comma makes the sentence confusing. Semicolons are necessary to clarify.

EXAMPLE 3

- Max bought a computer to play Overwatch, a shooting game that requires a top-notch graphic card; Sheila bought a computer to learn Korean through self-study; and John bought a computer to watch and manage his stocks. (O)

EXPLANATION Using semicolons makes it easier for you to comprehend the sentence. Now, let's see how this sentence becomes an SAT writing question.

EXAMPLE 4

- Max bought a computer to play ______ Sheila bought a computer to learn Korean through self-study; and John bought a computer to watch and manage his stocks.

  A) Overwatch, a shooting game that requires a top-notch graphic card,

  B) Overwatch, a shooting game that requires a top-notch graphic card;

  C) Overwatch; a shooting game that requires a top-notch graphic card,

  D) Overwatch a shooting game that requires a top-notch graphic card,

EXPLANATION This type of question becomes easier when you know the reason for the answer.

LESSON 4 **If the structures of the clauses within the sentence are the same, the repetitive words can be omitted.**

EXAMPLE

- Max bought a computer to play Overwatch, a shooting game that requires a top-notch graphic card; Sheila ~~bought a computer~~ to learn Korean through self-study; and John ~~bought a computer~~ to watch and manage his stocks.

- Max bought a computer to play Overwatch, a shooting game that requires a top-notch graphic card; Sheila to learn Korean through self-study; and John to watch and manage his stocks.

EXPLANATION The grammatical term for this concept is called ellipsis. If you were told semicolons are used to separate clauses or list more than 2 items, don't be shocked to see "seemingly" incomplete clauses or unparalleled lists. Some of the words are just omitted because they are redundant.

Building skill for solving the actual questions

SCENARIO 1 **Look at the answer choices first and if you spot a semi-colon, then the question is about identifying whether the sentence has one or two independent clauses.**

EXAMPLE Mr. Kim practices dancing every ________ that one day he will become a popular dancer.

A) day, believing

B) day: believing

C) day; believing

D) day. Believing

Step 1

If you spot a semicolon and period in the answer choices, you can eliminate both of them since they are interchangeable.

Step 2

The information that precedes the colon does not equate or define what comes after, and the sentence contains only one independent clause. Therefore, the answer is A.

SCENARIO 2

If you spot "; and" in a sentence, you should know there is a list, meaning that another semicolon (;) should be somewhere before the "; and."

Also, the list of items should be parallel, so when there is "A, B, and C", look for B or C to see how the structure is organized.

EXAMPLE

The suspects for the murder of the 42-year-old crime reporter were __________ Tony, the janitor; and Sheila, the principal of the school.

A) John, the teacher,

B) John, the teacher;

C) John; the teacher;

D) John the teacher

Step 1

There is "; and" so you should eliminate answer choice A and D because it does not have another semicolon.

Step 2

Decide which part of the list you should look for. In this case, A is blank, and B is partly missing(blank). So you should pick part C of the list which is after "; and."

Step 3

Look how the structure of the list is organized - "Name, appositive."

Step 4

Pick the answer choice that is parallel to list C. The answer is B.

SEMICOLON DRILL

Answers are provided on page 206.

INSTRUCTION

Each sentence has two independent clauses. Divide them using a semicolon.

EXAMPLE

weather; however,

- The concert was canceled due to bad **weather, however,** the organizers quickly rescheduled it for next week.

1

The serene stillness of the evening enveloped the landscape, creating a peaceful atmosphere, residents strolled along the quiet streets, enjoying the tranquility of the moment.

2

The potential contamination of rainwater with uranium, resulting from the release of supposedly-treated radioactive water, raises notable environmental and health concerns, proper scrutiny, monitoring, and effective treatment methods are crucial to mitigate the risks associated with this issue and protect both the ecosystem and human health.

3

The release of toxic pollutants into the air from industrial emissions poses substantial environmental and public health risks, implementing strict emission standards is an essential measure to mitigate these concerns and protect both the environment and the well-being of nearby communities.

4

Inspired by her personal experiences, renowned author Maya Angelou dedicated herself to advocating for civil rights and social justice throughout her life. Her tireless work included delivering powerful speeches, penning influential books, and using her creative talents to shed light on the struggles faced by marginalized communities.

5

Considering the higher occurrence of a particular enzyme variant in individuals with a heightened sense of taste, some researchers suggest that its function is not passive rather, it may actively contribute to the perception and discrimination of flavors.

EM-DASH (-)

WHAT IS EM-DASH

The em-dash(–) is often used to indicate a break in thought or to set apart parenthetical information within a sentence.

LESSON 1

Just like commas, the em-dash can frame nonrestrictive elements – appositives and modifiers.

EXAMPLE

- Doctors are increasingly collaborating with each other, a trend highlighted by the rise in the number of medical research papers with multiple authors. (O)
- Doctors are increasingly collaborating with each other—a trend highlighted by the rise in the number of medical research papers with multiple authors. (O)

- The new employee—fresh out of college and with little work experience, impressed the company with his innovative ideas and willingness to learn. (X)
- The new employee, fresh out of college and with little work experience—impressed the company with his innovative ideas and willingness to learn. (X)
- The new employee, fresh out of college and with little work experience, impressed the company with his innovative ideas and willingness to learn. (O)
- The new employee—fresh out of college and with little work experience—impressed the company with his innovative ideas and willingness to learn. (O)

EXPLANATION

Remember! If a nonrestrictive element is in the middle, either commas or em-dashes should be paired to frame it. On the SAT, hyphens(shorter lines) are often used between those dashes to confuse test takers.

LESSON 2 **The em-dash can introduce various structures to indicate a break in thought or give additional information.**

EXAMPLE

- Despite the long commute and hectic schedule, the new job was a dream come true—with exciting projects and great colleagues to work with.
- The winding roads of California's Pacific Coast Highway offer stunning views of the ocean—in some places, the cliffs drop straight down to the water.
- At just ten years old, she submitted a poem to a local contest—and took home the first prize.
- In many species of turtles, sex is determined by the temperature of the eggs during a critical period of development—warmer temperatures produce females, while cooler temperatures produce males.
- The small town of Bethlehem, Pennsylvania is known for its vibrant arts scene—in addition to hosting an annual music festival, it boasts numerous galleries and theaters.

Building skills to solve the actual questions

SCENARIO 1 **When you read along the sentence and see two em-dashes, it is not a dash question.**

EXAMPLE

The new employee—fresh out of college and with little work experience—______ the company with his innovative ideas and willingness to learn.

A) impressed

B) impressing

C) have impressed

D) to impress

Step 1

You can just cross out what is framed in those two dashes.

Step 2

You can simply see that the subject is *employee*(singular) and a verb is needed. B and D are not verbs, and C is plural. Therefore, the answer is A.

SCENARIO 2 **You read along the sentence and see only one em-dash; then you spot an em-dash from the answer choices.**

EXAMPLE Despite the long commute and hectic schedule, the new job was a dream come true—with exciting projects and great ________ work with.

A) colleagues to

B) colleagues: to

C) colleagues—to

D) colleagues, to

Step 1

Cross out what is framed in those two dashes and see if it makes sense. Despite the long commute and hectic schedule, the new job was a dream come true—~~with exciting projects and great colleagues~~—to work with.

Step 2

The phrase "to work with" modifies the "projects" and "colleagues," not the "new job." So you cannot just partially leave the phrase "to work with" out. You can eliminate answer choice C. A colon or comma is not needed. Therefore, the answer is A.

SCENARIO 3 **You read along the sentence and see only one em-dash; then you spot an em-dash from the answer choices.**

EXAMPLE The storm was raging outside—thunder booming, lightning __________ inside, with a warm blanket and a good book, I felt cozy and content.

A) Flashing. But

B) flashing—but

C) flashing; but

D) flashing but

Step 1

Cross out what is framed in those two dashes and see if it makes sense. In this sentence, two independent clauses are separated by the conjunction "but." The em dash sets up a contrast between the raging storm outside and the cozy feeling inside, and the word "but" adds to this contrast by introducing the idea of unexpected coziness despite the storm.

Step 2

You should not choose answer choices that a coordinating junction starts a sentence or separates two sentences without a comma. Eliminate A and D. When you spot a semicolon with a coordinating conjunction, there should be a list. Eliminate C. Therefore, the answer is B.

COLON (:)

WHAT IS COLON

A colon is used to introduce a list or a lengthy explanation that follows an independent clause.

LESSON 1

Use colons when you went to equate or explain a word, phrase, or clause.

EXAMPLE

- I have three siblings: John, Mary, and David.
  (siblings = John, Mary, and David)
- She had only one goal in life: to travel the world and see all its wonders.
  (one goal= to travel the world and see all its wonders)
- The situation was dire: they had no food or water left.
  (the situation was dire = they had no food or water left)

LESSON 2

Do not use colons immediately after expressions like "such as," "including," or "for example."

EXAMPLE

- Alice has many books, ***including***: classic literature, contemporary fiction, and biographies. (X)
- Alice has many books, ***including*** classic literature, contemporary fiction, and biographies. (O)
- I enjoy reading books in different genres, ***such as***: mystery, romance, and science fiction. (X)
- I enjoy reading books in different genres, ***such as*** mystery, romance, and science fiction. (O)

LESSON 3

Do not use colons when a title (usually italicized) follows a noun.

EXAMPLE

- Banksy left a profound impact on the art world with his work **piece**: *A Flower Thrower.* (X)
- Banksy left a profound impact on the art world with his work **piece** *A Flower Thrower. (O)*

Building skills to solve the actual questions

** Parentheses are used to set off or enclose modifiers.*

SCENARIO 1 **You spot semicolons along with other punctuations or conjunctions in the answer choices.**

EXAMPLE A report released by nutritionist Sarah Brown in 2021 provides a new perspective on the benefits of eating ______ called phytosterols, cholesterol-like molecules that contribute to maintaining healthy cholesterol levels when consumed as part of a balanced diet.

A) nuts compounds

B) nuts: compounds

C) nuts; compounds

D) nuts, while compounds

Step 1

Before selecting the punctuation based on the context, check the sentence structure first. See if there is an independent clause before and after the word *nuts*.

*A **report** (released by nutritionist Sarah Brown in 2021) **provides** a new perspective (on the benefits of eating nuts) compounds (called phytosterols), (cholesterol-like molecules) (that contribute to maintaining healthy cholesterol levels when consumed as part of a balanced diet.)*

Report is the subject, ***provides*** the verb, and ***a new perspective*** the object.

Step2

Now, tackle the answer choices.

A) nuts compounds: This option lacks punctuation between "nuts" and "compounds." It connects the two words with a space, suggesting that "nuts compounds" is a single phrase. However, this doesn't fit the context of the sentence, which describes the benefits of eating something related to nuts.

B) nuts: compounds: This option uses a colon between "nuts" and "compounds." A colon is often used to introduce a list, explanation, or elaboration. In this case, the colon implies that "compounds" will further specify the type of nuts mentioned in the sentence.

C) nuts; compounds: This option uses a semicolon between "nuts" and "compounds." A semicolon is typically used to connect independent clauses or separate items in a list when there are commas within the items. Neither is applied in this case. The word called is a participle, not a verb.

D) nuts, while compounds: This option uses a comma followed by the conjunction "while." This choice also needs a clause, but a verb is missing. Check the contextual aspect only when there is no grammatical error.

The answer is B.

SCENARIO 2 **You spot semicolons along with other punctuations or conjunctions in the answer choices.**

EXAMPLE

An article published in the Journal of Psychology by researcher John Doe in 2018 provides evidence that meditation can improve mental ______ participants who meditated for at least 10 minutes a day reported lower levels of anxiety and depression compared to those who did not meditate.

A) health:

B) health,

C) health, while

D) health while

Step 1

Analyze Sentence Structure:
Before selecting punctuation based on context, examine the sentence structure to identify any grammatical issues. Specifically, check if there's an independent clause before and after the word *"health."*

*An **article** (published in the Journal of Psychology by researcher John Doe in 2018)*

***provides** evidence (that meditation can improve mental health)______ **participants** (who meditated for at least 10 minutes a day) **reported** lower levels of anxiety and depression compared to those who did not meditate.*

The clause *"that meditation can improve mental health"* is a noun clause that clarifies or modifies *"evidence."*

In this sentence, ***"article"*** is the subject, and ***"provides"*** is the verb in the first clause, while ***"participants"*** is the subject and ***"reported"*** is the verb in the second clause.

Step 2

Evaluate Answer Choices:
B) health, This choice places a comma after "health." However, this creates a comma splice by joining two independent clauses without a conjunction, which is incorrect.

Since both the colon (:) and the conjunction ***"while"*** can connect two clauses, let's assess the choices contextually. The fact that participants report lower anxiety does not show contrast with the article's claim of evidence, nor does it imply a simultaneous action. Thus, choices C and D are unsuitable.

The answer is A. Here, the colon effectively introduces the evidence discussed in the first part of the sentence.

APOSTROPHE(')

WHAT IS AN APOSTROPHE

An apostrophe is a punctuation mark used for various purposes: contractions and possession.

LESSON 1 **Use apostrophes to show contractions—when letters are omitted in words.**

EXAMPLE

- John's going to sleep soon. = John is
- We're not dating. = We are
- They've always encouraged me in everything. = They have

EXPLANATION Those are the common contractions we make.

LESSON 2 **Be cautious with commonly confused contractions on the SAT.**

EXAMPLE

It's = it is	It's awesome.
Its = possessive form	Don't judge the book by its cover.
Its' = incorrect grammar	
They're = they are	They're having fun.
Their = Possessive form	Hedgehogs do not have sharp spines on their face.
There = location	You should not leave your wallet there.
You're = You are	I believe that you're great.
Your = possessive form	Always tidy your bed when you wake up.

LESSON 3 **Use apostrophes to show possession.**

EXAMPLE

- John's new computer is expensive.
- My dog's hair is all over my room. (I have only one dog)
- My dogs' hair is all over my room. (I have more than one dog)

EXPLANATION Adding apostrophes to singular or plural nouns depends on the context of its passage.

LESSON 4 **To use a possessive form for a nonhuman noun, it must precede another noun because a nonhuman element cannot claim its ownership.**

EXAMPLE

- The desk's color is blue, and its ***legs'*** is red. (X)
- The desk's color is blue, and its ***legs' color*** is red. (O)
- A substantial portion of student's ***success'*** can be attributed to the unwavering support provided by dedicated parents or guardians. (X)
- A substantial portion of student's ***success*** can be attributed to the unwavering support provided by dedicated parents or guardians. (O)

PUNCTUATION PROBLEM SET

Answers are provided on page 206.

1

The 250 ancient temples of Cambodia's Angkor Wat are maintained through a process known as stone conservation, where rainfall and humidity gradually erode the structures, and preservationists delicately restore them—in this case, the sandstone blocks of the ________ maintain their historical integrity.

Which choice completes the text so that it conforms to the conventions of Standard English?

A) edifices to

B) edifices: to

C) edifices—to

D) edifices, to

2

As long as educational institutions continue to expect high performance from ________ should advocate for balanced school-life schedules as a way to keep students motivated, healthy, and successful.

Which choice completes the text so that it conforms to the conventions of Standard English?

A) students, administrators

B) students; administrators

C) students, administrators,

D) students, administrators

3

Tea is consumed in India in many ways, either pure or with diverse mixtures of spices, and each variant has a unique name. A tea infused with cardamom, cloves, and cinnamon ________ while tea with milk and sugar, but no spices, is often referred to as chai.

Which choice completes the text so that it conforms to the conventions of Standard English?

A) is a masala chai: for instance,

B) is a masala chai, for instance:

C) is, a masala chai for instance—

D) is a masala chai, for instance,

4

Annually, several types of whales move from feeding grounds in the polar regions to warmer breeding waters in the ________ of thousands of miles that involves frequent pauses to rest and eat.

Which choice completes the text so that it conforms to the conventions of Standard English?

A) Tropics. A voyage

B) tropics, a voyage

C) tropics; a voyage

D) tropics; which is a voyage

5

The danger of malfunction is considerable, and the outer space is a hostile environment for most of the ________ satellites never fail to complete their scheduled orbits.

Which choice completes the text so that it conforms to the conventions of Standard English?

A) time; yet the

B) time: yet the

C) time, the

D) time, yet the

6

As software engineers started to appreciate the lead developer's elegant coding ________ in turn began to experiment with implementing innovative coding strategies of their own.

Which choice completes the text so that it conforms to the conventions of Standard English?

A) solutions; they

B) solutions, they

C) solutions they

D) solutions. They

7

Vertical ________ was praised as an eco-friendly method to save water-intensive crops such as lettuce, herbs, and tomatoes while satisfying the human need for fresh produce.

Which choice completes the text so that it conforms to the conventions of Standard English?

A) farming, or aeroponics,

B) farming—or aeroponics,

C) farming, or aeroponics

D) farming or aeroponics

8

The research, the most extensive ever conducted on meditation and wellbeing, confirmed a definite—though still not fully ________ correlation between regular meditation and experiencing a more peaceful, healthier life.

Which choice completes the text so that it conforms to the conventions of Standard English?

A) understood—

B) understood;

C) understood,

D) understood

9

On April 26, 1986, the world witnessed one of the worst Nuclear Power Plant. This disastrous nuclear incident contaminated the bustling town of ________ with lethal amounts of radiation and fallout.

Which choice completes the text so that it conforms to the conventions of Standard English?

A) Pripyat near Chernobyl, Ukraine,

B) Pripyat, near Chernobyl, Ukraine

C) Pripyat, near Chernobyl, Ukraine,

D) Pripyat–near Chernobyl, Ukraine,

10

India's Taj Mahal has been combating air pollution damage since industrial development intensified in Agra over 50 years ago. Indeed, if the monument's preservation had not involved considerable efforts to reduce air pollution and carry out regular cleaning, the ________ would likely have discolored more extensively.

Which choice completes the text so that it conforms to the conventions of Standard English?

A) Taj Mahal's white marble façade's

B) Taj Mahal's white marble's façade

C) Taj Mahals white marble façade

D) Taj Mahal's white marble façade

11

Workplace wellness initiatives suggest that employers offer their ________ to maintain physical health and mental well-being. According to human resources expert Laura Hamill, such programs can attract candidates who value personal health and work-life balance.

Which choice completes the text so that it conforms to the conventions of Standard English?

A) employees programs

B) employees' programs

C) employee's program's

D) employees programs'

12

While UNESCO works to protect sites classified as World Heritage, ________ that do not appear on the organization's World Heritage list.

Which choice completes the text so that it conforms to the conventions of Standard English?

A) historians' have identified numerous culturally significant locations

B) historians' have identified numerous culturally significant locations

C) historians have identified numerous culturally significant locations'

D) historians have identified numerous culturally significant locations

7

QUESTION TYPE APPROACH

- ❒ SUBJECT & VERB AGREEMENT
- ❒ RUN-ON & FRAGMENT
- ❒ COMPARISON
- ❒ PARALLELISM
- ❒ PRONOUN AGREEMENT
- ❒ SUBJUNCTIVE MOOD
- ❒ TRANSITION
- ❒ DANGLING MODIFIER
- ❒ BOUNDARIES
- ❒ RHETORICAL SYNTHESIS

SUBJECT & VERB AGREEMENT

LESSON 1

To ensure correct subject-verb agreement, accurately identify the subject and the verb in a sentence. Ignore modifiers that come between the subject and the verb. On the SAT, test makers often separate the subject and verb to confuse test-takers.

Modifiers can include prepositional phrases, appositives, participial phrases, and relative clauses. If you are unfamiliar with these terms, please refer to the appropriate chapters for more information.

EXAMPLE

- The rapid **expansion** ~~of e-commerce in recent years, driven by the increasing demand for online shopping and the convenience of home delivery,~~ **has transformed** the retail industry and **posed** new challenges for traditional brick-and-mortar stores.

- The intricate **interplay** ~~between genetic predisposition, environmental factors, and lifestyle choices, which can significantly impact an individual's risk of developing chronic diseases,~~ **underscores** the complexity of modern healthcare and **highlights** the importance of personalized medicine.

LESSON 2

Be cautious with certain prepositional phrases such as *as well as*, *in addition to*, and *along with*. These phrases do not make the subject plural; they act as modifiers.

EXAMPLE

- **Mark** ~~as well as Max~~ **is** attending the conference.
- **Mark** and **Max are** attending the conference.
- **Sarah** ~~along with her brother~~ **was going** to the store to buy groceries.

EXPLANATION

As long as the words are not connected with coordinating junctions, you should regard those phrases as modifiers.

LESSON 3

There are tricky conjunctions: *not only A but also B*, *either A or B*, and *neither A nor B*. Whatever is closer to the verb should be regarded as the subject- in most cases, *B*.

EXAMPLE

- Not only Sarah but also her **sisters enjoy** playing soccer in their free time.
- Neither her sisters nor **Sara has** ever traveled outside the country.
- **Neither** of Sara's sisters **has** ever traveled outside the country.

EXPLANATION

When ***neither*** or ***either*** is used without ***nor*** or ***or***, they are singular and require a singular verb.

LESSON 4

Indefinite pronouns such as *some*, *most*, *all*, *none*, and *any* can be singular or plural depending on the noun they refer to.

EXAMPLE

- **Some** of the **characters** in Gulliver's Travels **were** fantastical creatures, such as the Houyhnhnms, a race of highly intelligent horses, and the Yahoos, primitive and brutish humanoid creatures.
- **Some** of the radioactive **water** from Fukushima **is** planned to be released into the Pacific Ocean.

LESSON 5

When dealing with gerund phrases as subjects, consider whether they are singular or plural based on context.

EXAMPLE

- **Making friends has** become more challenging in the age of social media and virtual communication. – The gerund phrase *Making friends* acts as a singular noun.
- **Exercising every day and making the bed every morning are** <u>two</u> simple <u>habits</u> that can have a significant positive impact on your physical and mental well-being.
- **Releasing radioactive water and touting it as safe to drink** <u>is</u> a dangerous and unethical <u>practice</u> that can have serious health consequences for those who consume it.

EXPLANATION

When there are two gerund phrases, don't just count them as plural. You need to see the latter part of the sentence. The second example says they are "two habits" so you know it's plural. But look at the third example. Two actions are counted as one by saying "a practice." In this case, a singular verb should be used.

LESSON 6 ***The number of*** **is singular whereas *a number of* is plural.**

EXAMPLE

- *The* ***number*** *of* aliens planning to communicate with us ***remains*** unknown.
- ***A number of*** Korean independence activists ***have been recognized*** and ***honored*** for their contributions to the country's independence movement.

EXPLANATION Normally, the object of a preposition cannot be a subject in a sentence because a prepositional phrase (preposition + its object) is a modifier. However, there is an exception to this rule: the phrase "a number of" acts as one word – some. So the second example can also read, "Some Korean independence **activists have been recognized** and **honored** for their contributions to the country's independence movement."

LESSON 7 **In inverted sentences, the verb comes before the subject. Inversions occur in the following situations:**

1. When we use *there* or a *preposition* equivalent to there at the beginning of a sentence.
2. When starting with negative words such as hardly, never, not only, only then, and little.
3. When beginning with a participle phrase for emphasis.
4. When using the subjunctive mood without *if.*

EXAMPLE

- There ***is*** a ***pen***. = On the desk ***is*** a ***pen***.
- ***Not*** until I got a perfect score on the SAT ***did I feel*** confident enough to apply to the most competitive universities in the country
- ***Planted*** hundred years ago ***were*** the majestic oak ***trees*** that now line the main street of our town.
- I would be sad ***had I*** not ***married*** you. = I would be sad if ***I had*** not **married** you.

SUBJECT & VERB DRILL

Answers are provided on page 207.

INSTRUCTION

Underline the subjects once in the following sentences and circle the right verbs.

1. Devastated by war and displacement, the resilient communities, with their vibrant cultures and deep-rooted traditions, (is/are) now striving for recovery and rebuilding.

2. The number of students enrolled in the university (has/have) steadily increased over the past decade, with over 30,000 students currently attending.

3. Against the wall (hangs/hang) several paintings that caught everyone's attention.

4. Both Daniel, who is an accomplished pianist, and Sarah, who is a skilled violinist, (has/have) met the conductor to discuss their upcoming collaboration in order to meet the high artistic expectations of the upcoming performance.

5. The long-term benefits of a healthy diet on physical and mental health (is/are) well documented by scientific studies.

6 The harmful effects of prolonged sitting on posture and musculoskeletal health (is/are) increasingly well documented by medical research.

7 Beside the fireplace (sits/sit) the family dogs, warming themselves on a cold winter evening.

8 Severely impacted by overfishing and climate change, the once teeming fish populations, with their shimmering scales and graceful movements, (is/are) now experiencing a steady decline.

9 The positive effects of mindfulness meditation on stress reduction and emotional regulation (is/are) becoming increasingly well documented by scientific studies.

10 The Palace of Versailles, a sumptuous royal residence built in the 17th century, (is/are) located just outside of Paris and is one of the most popular tourist attractions in France.

11 Beneath the surface of the water (swims/swim) graceful dolphins.

12 The Acropolis, a citadel and ancient monument located in Athens, Greece, (overlooks/overlook) the city and offers stunning views of the surrounding landscape.

13 Surprisingly little (is/are) known about the long-term effects of social media on mental health despite its widespread use among people of all ages.

14 On the edge of the cliff (stands/stand) tourists taking photos.

15 Ravaged by wildfires and deforestation, the lush rainforests, adorned with a rich diversity of plant and animal species, (is/are) now facing the risk of irreversible destruction.

16 Devastated by war and displacement, the resilient communities, with their vibrant cultures and deep-rooted traditions, (is/are) now striving for recovery and rebuilding.

17 Near the entrance to the park (sits/sit) homeless men begging for spare change.

18 Deeply affected by pollution and habitat loss, the delicate coral reefs, adorned with vibrant colors and intricate formations, (is/are) now displaying early signs of regeneration.

19 Sarah's paintings of the coastal landscapes (reflects/reflect) a profound fascination with and appreciation for the ever-changing colors and textures of the sea.

20 From the top of the mountains (comes/come) a loud, piercing scream every day.

21 The number of people living in poverty (has/have) decreased significantly in many parts of the world due to various government programs and economic growth.

RUN-ON & FRAGMENT

LESSON 1

In order to join two clauses, you need one conjunction. What if you want to join 3 clauses? Then 2 conjunctions are needed.

Think of a train. How many joints are needed to connect 5 cars?

You need 4 connectors. The same applies to joining clauses.

Two cars without a connector will not move together.

A **run-on sentence** occurs when two or more clauses are joined without proper punctuation or conjunctions. A **comma splice** is a type of run-on sentence where clauses are incorrectly joined by a comma.

Let's say you come across a sentence that has two clauses without a conjunction.

There are several ways to correct run-on sentences.

1. Insert period to end one clause and capitalize the first letter of the other clause.
2. Insert a conjunction.
3. Insert a semicolon.
4. If the latter clause defines the previous one, then insert a colon.

EXAMPLE

- Mike likes to study he often finds it difficult to concentrate for long periods of time. (Run-on)
- Mike likes to study, he often finds it difficult to concentrate for long periods of time. (Comma-splice)
- Mike likes to study, but he often finds it difficult to concentrate for long periods of time. (a coordinating conjunction is inserted.)
- Mike, who likes to study, often finds it difficult to concentrate for long periods of time. (a relative clause conjunction is inserted.)
- Mike likes to study; however, he often finds it difficult to concentrate for long periods of time. (A semicolon is inserted. *However* is not a conjunction. It is a conjunctive adverb.)
- I have a busy day ahead of me: I need to finish my work project, go grocery shopping, and attend a doctor's appointment. (without the colon, it would be a run-on sentence)

LESSON 2

Using more conjunctions than necessary is grammatically incorrect and leads to conjunction redundancy.

EXAMPLE

- ***Although*** Mike likes to study, ***but*** he often finds it difficult to concentrate for long periods of time. (X)
- ~~***Although***~~ Mike likes to study, ***but*** he often finds it difficult to concentrate for long periods of time. (O)
- ***Although*** Mike likes to study, ~~***but***~~ he often finds it difficult to concentrate for long periods of time. (O)

EXPLANATION

In order to join two clauses, only one conjunction is needed. Just remember one equation:

# of clauses – 1 = # of conjunctions

LESSON 3

A fragment is an incomplete sentence that lacks a subject, a verb, or does not express a complete thought. Fragments can also be dependent clauses that are not connected to an independent clause.

EXAMPLE

- Although I studied hard for the test.
  (It needs an independent clause or *although* should be erased)
- In the middle of the night, when the moon was full.
  (It needs an independent clause or *when* should be erased)
- A tall, dark-haired stranger with piercing blue eyes.
  (It is a noun phrase. A verb is needed.)
- After finishing my homework, watching TV for an hour.
  (A subject and a verb is missing.)
- Eating breakfast in the morning, drinking coffee.
  (Two gerund phrases-noun phrases- are written. You can use them to make a sentence.)

RUN-ON & FRAGMENT DRILL

Answers are provided on page 208.

INSTRUCTION **Identify whether the sentence is run-on, fragment, or conjunction redundancy.**

1. The soccer team had a strong start to the season, they won first few matches in impressive fashion.

2. Racing against the clock, trying to finish the report, feeling overwhelmed with tasks.

3. Shopping for groceries, forgot my wallet, left my list at home.

4. Rushing through the crowd, searching for the exit, hoping to catch the last train.

5. Lexy loves to dance John prefers to sing they have different hobbies but enjoy each other's company.

6. The new restaurant was bustling with activity, customers eagerly sampled the eclectic menu and lively atmosphere.

7. Because Isabella forgot her umbrella, so she got soaked in the rain.

8. The weather was beautiful we decided to go for a hike and then have a picnic at the park.

9 I went to the store to buy groceries I ended up buying way more than I needed and spent way too much money.

10 Running late for the meeting, without my coffee, in need of a break.

11 Juggling multiple projects, answering emails, attending meetings, all while managing a tight deadline.

12 While Betty was studying for her exams, but her phone kept buzzing with notifications.

13 I woke up late this morning I rushed to get ready but missed the bus.

14 When Jake needs to finish this project by tomorrow.

15 The concert was incredible because the band played all their hit songs, the crowd went wild.

16 Nate studied for hours his hard work paid off when he aced the exam.

17 Skyler loves to travel she has been to over 20 countries and plans to visit many more in the future.

18 Although Keisha had practiced for hours, but she still struggled to play the piano piece flawlessly.

COMPARISON

WHAT IS COMPARISON

When making a comparison, it is important to be careful to avoid making false or misleading comparisons.

LESSON 1

A comparison should be clear about which elements are being compared. The law of proximity states that readers naturally associate words that are close together.

EXAMPLE 1

- *I* can run faster than ***John***.

EXPLANATION The comparison is between ***I*** and ***John*** because ***John*** is the closest noun to ***I***.

EXAMPLE 2

- *I* like John more than ***Mike***.

EXPLANATION Who is being compared with Mike this time? Is it John or I? Since *John* is closer to *Mike*, the sentence should be understood as *I like John more than I like Mike*, comparing *John* with *Mike*. What should be done to compare *Mike* with *I*? Add a verb to make *Mike* a subject.

EXAMPLE 3

- *I* like John more than ***Mike*** does.

EXPLANATION In that way, the sentence can now be understood as *I like John more than Mike likes John,* comparing *I* with *Mike*. But the sentence on the SAT will be trickier.

EXAMPLE 4

- The newly made electronic robots produce more ***cars*** than ***machines*** that are powered by gasoline. (X)
- The newly made electronic ***robots*** produce more cars than do ***machines*** that are powered by gasoline. (O)

EXPLANATION Contextually, you will have no problem comprehending the sentence. However, the sentence is ambiguous because it compares ***cars*** to ***machines***. Since ***robots*** do not produce ***machines***, '***machines***' should be made the subject with an added verb. If a modifier is present, inversion may occur, as shown in this example.

LESSON 2 **Ensure that the things being compared are similar in nature or scope.**

EXAMPLE

- The energy consumption of this new model is significantly lower than the previous version. (X)
- The energy consumption of this new model is significantly lower than that of the previous version. (O)

EXPLANATION

In the first example, the comparison is incorrectly made between ***energy consumption*** and ***the previous version***, which is illogical. Using ***that of*** refers back to ***energy consumption***, making the comparison logical.

Use ***that of*** for singular nouns and ***those of*** for plural nouns to avoid illogical comparisons.

LESSON 3

Comparative: **Used when comparing two things.**
Formed by adding *-er* or using *more*.

Superlative: **Used when comparing three or more things.**
Formed by adding *-est* or using *most*.

EXAMPLE

- My cat is faster than your cat.
- My cat is the fastest cat in the neighborhood.

LESSON 4

For countable nouns:
Comparative: Use *fewer* or *more*.
Superlative: Use *fewest* or *most*.

For uncountable nouns:
Comparative: Use *less* or *more*.
Superlative: Use *least* or *most*.

EXAMPLE

- Countable Nouns:
  There are *more* apples in the basket than pears.
  This basket has the ***most*** apples of all the baskets.
- Uncountable Nouns:
  This coffee has ***less*** caffeine than that one.
  That coffee has the ***most*** caffeine of all the ones we tried.

COMPARISON PROBLEM SET

Answers are provided on page 208~209.

1

Many individuals opt for electric vehicles because they believe that EVs offer a greener and more sustainable mode of transportation ______________ which contribute to air pollution and greenhouse gas emissions.

Which choice completes the text so that it conforms to the conventions of Standard English?

A) than the selection of traditional gasoline-powered cars,

B) than selecting traditional gasoline-powered cars,

C) than do traditional gasoline-powered cars,

D) than the people who select traditional gasoline-powered cars,

2

The educational journey for dental hygienists is considerably shorter than ___________ with dental hygienists typically completing their training in two to three years, whereas dentists go through a more extensive process lasting around seven to eight years.

Which choice completes the text so that it conforms to the conventions of Standard English?

A) that of dentists,

B) those of dentists,

C) that compared with dentists,

D) dentists,

3

Evidence strongly suggests that Megalosaurus thrived in what is now the eastern part of England, an area that was once as lush and fertile as ______________

Which choice completes the text so that it conforms to the conventions of Standard English?

A) where the Amazon rainforest region is.

B) those of the Amazon rainforest region.

C) the Amazon rainforest.

D) what the Amazon rainforest is like.

4

The research findings unveiled that individuals who reported consuming berries a minimum of five times per week were 15 percent less likely to experience cognitive decline over a five-year period than ______________ consumption.

Which choice completes the text so that it conforms to the conventions of Standard English?

A) when people had no berry

B) if people reported they had no berry

C) those who reported no berry

D) no berry

5

Scientists conducting a study in Oregon discovered that middle school students who engaged in hands-on robotics projects scored 4.9 points higher on a mathematics proficiency exam____________ in such activities.

Which choice completes the text so that it conforms to the conventions of Standard English?

A) the scores of students who did not participate

B) not-participating students' scores

C) those of students not participating

D) did students who did not participate

6

During the Renaissance, artists like Leonardo da Vinci and Michelangelo revolutionized the world of visual arts by exploring new techniques and pushing the boundaries of artistic expression ____________

Which choice completes the text so that it conforms to the conventions of Standard English?

A) more than preceding eras had.

B) more than artists of preceding eras had.

C) more than that in preceding eras.

D) more than preceding eras.

7

That Chris received a scholarship for his academic achievements surprised those of us who believed that his performance was significantly inferior to ____________ who had excelled in multiple areas of study.

Which choice completes the text so that it conforms to the conventions of Standard English?

A) other candidates

B) that of other candidates

C) those of other candidates

D) those

8

Unlike nocturnal animals, whose eyes are often adapted for low-light conditions, ____________

Which choice completes the text so that it conforms to the conventions of Standard English?

A) the eyes of diurnal animals are generally well-suited for daylight vision and color perception.

B) It is general for the eyes of diurnal animals to be well-suited for daylight vision and color perception.

C) diurnal animals generally possess eyes that are well-suited for daylight vision and color perception.

D) well-suited eyes for daylight vision and color perception are general of diurnal animals.

ELLIPSIS

WHAT IS ELLIPSIS

Ellipsis is the omission of one or more words from a sentence or phrase that are not necessary for the sentence to be grammatically complete or understandable. The omitted words are typically implied or understood based on context.

LESSON 1

Ellipsis is often used to avoid repetition or to make sentences more concise, especially when the structures of the clauses or phrases within the sentence are same. It can occur in various parts of a sentence, including the omission of verbs, nouns, pronouns, articles, or other parts of speech.

Think of a simplification in Math:

$$2x + 2y = 2(x+y)$$

EXAMPLE 1

- **I** go to school, and **I** meet my friends.

  ➡ I go to school and meet my friends.

EXAMPLE 2

- Back in the old days, people **would** communicate through handwritten letters and **would** eagerly wait for the mailman's arrival, hoping for news from distant friends and family.

  ➡ Back in the old days, people **would** communicate through handwritten letters and eagerly wait for the mailman's arrival, hoping for news from distant friends and family.

EXAMPLE 3

- The classification of a substance as **a** hazardous material, **a** toxic chemical, or **an**other regulated compound can impose restrictions on handling and disposal practices.

  ➡ The classification of a substance as **a** hazardous material, toxic chemical, or other regulated compound can impose restrictions on handling and disposal practices.

EXAMPLE 4

- Max and Tessa **practice dancing**, and Max **practice dancing** to lose weight, and Tessa **practice dancing** to enter a dance competition.

  ➡ Max and Tessa **practice dancing,** Max to lose weight and Tessa to enter a dance competition.

EXAMPLE 5

- **If she is** generous, **she is criticized as being** naive; **if she is** forgiving, **she is criticized as** being weak.

  ➡ **If she is** generous, **she is criticized as being** naive; **if** forgiving, **being** weak.

EXPLANATION **Words like "she is" are omitted but understood from context.**

LESSON 2 **Ellipsis often occurs in comparative sentences to avoid repetition.**

EXAMPLE 1

- John **can run** faster than I **can run**.

  ➡ John can run faster than I.

EXAMPLE 2

- **John likes** Betty more than **John likes** Alison.

  ➡ John likes Betty more than Alison.

EXPLANATION **The two elements compared are Betty and Alison.**

EXAMPLE 3

- John **likes Betty** more than Alison **likes Betty.**

  ➡ John likes Betty more than Alison **does.**

EXPLANATION **In this case, you need to indicate that *Alison* is the subject by adding a verb to it so that the readers know the two elements compared to are two subjects: John and Alison.**

PARALLELISM

Parallelism involves using the same grammatical structure for similar elements within a sentence, creating balance and clarity.

LESSON 1 **When joining words or phrases with a conjunction, ensure they are in the same grammatical form.**

EXAMPLE

- Mary likes ***to swim*** and ***dancing***. (X)
- Mary likes ***swimming*** and ***dancing***. (O)
- Mary likes ***to swim*** and ***to dance***. (O)
- Mary likes to ***swim*** and ***dance***. (O)

EXPLANATION *To swim* is in an infinitive form but *dancing* is in a gerund form. You can change either of them to make it in the same form. As for the last sentence, you can just join what is different as you simplify a math equation: ax+ay= a(x+y)

LESSON 2 **In lists of three or more items, maintain the same grammatical structure for each item.**

EXAMPLE

- I bought ***apples***, ***bananas***, and ***I found oranges for my fruit salad***. (X)
- I bought ***apples***, ***bananas***, and ***oranges*** for my fruit salad. (O)

EXPLANATION All items ("apples," "bananas," "oranges") are nouns in a list.

LESSON 3 **When a sentence has a subject and a predicate nominative, they should be in the same form.**

EXAMPLE

- ***To listen to others*** is ***gaining wisdom***. (X)
- ***To listen to others*** is ***to gain wisdom***. (O)

EXPLANATION To *listen* is an infinitive, and *gaining* is a gerund.

Building skills to solve the actual questions

SCENARIO 1

You encounter a sentence with a list of items [A], [B], and [C] and need to choose what fits for [C].

EXAMPLE

Jeffrey's goal for the new year is to exercise every day, to eat breakfast, and ________.

A) waking up early in the morning
B) is to wake up early in the morning
C) to wake up early in the morning
D) another goal is to wake up early in the morning

Step 1

When the last item [C] is missing, focus on the second item [B], especially what part of speech comes after right the comma. In this case, the infinitive phrase ***to eat*** is the second item, so you can match the answer choice with it. The Answer is C.

SCENARIO 2 **You encounter answer choices that have commas in different places. You know it is a listing question and need to correctly divide the listing.**

EXAMPLE Spinoza was dedicated to developing a systematic ________ and advocating for a society based on individual freedom

A) philosophy of nature emphasizing the importance of living a virtuous life,
B) philosophy of nature emphasizing the importance of living, a virtuous life,
C) philosophy of nature emphasizing, the importance of living a virtuous life,
D) philosophy of nature, emphasizing the importance of living a virtuous life,

Step 1

When the second item [B] or the first and second items ([A], [B]) are missing, focus on the last item [C] which comes right after the conjunction ***and***. In this case, the gerund phrase ***advocating*** is the last item, so you know the listing starts with the gerund. The three items listed in this sentence are developing, emphasizing, and advocating. Therefore, the answer is D.

PARALLELISM PROBLEM SET

Answers are provided on page 209.

1

With the increasing use of technology among children, many parents are turning to software that allows them to monitor their kids' online activities and ________ restrictions on screen time.

Which choice completes the text so that it conforms to the conventions of Standard English?

A) set

B) setting

C) sets

D) for setting

2

The coach urged the team to practice harder, to stay focused, and ________ their best effort in every game.

Which choice completes the text so that it conforms to the conventions of Standard English?

A) give

B) giving

C) to give

D) for giving

3

Although electric cars have gained popularity due to their environmental benefits, they still cannot match conventional vehicles in terms of long-distance travel, the availability of refueling infrastructure in many regions, and ________.

Which choice completes the text so that it conforms to the conventions of Standard English?

A) they do not have the convenience of fast refueling options

B) are not convenient because of lacking fast refueling options

C) the convenience of fast refueling options

D) about the convenient options of fast refueling

4

Smartphones with built-in high-resolution cameras became popular after the introduction of advanced imaging technology that eliminated the need not only for traditional film rolls but also ________.

Which choice completes the text so that it conforms to the conventions of Standard English?

A) separate digital cameras

B) to separate digital cameras

C) for separate digital cameras

D) separate cameras that are digital.

5

Frustrated with the upcoming exams, Sarah decided to stop spending time on looking at her social networking sites and ________ her energy towards intensive studying.

Which choice completes the text so that it conforms to the conventions of Standard English?

A) redirect

B) redirecting

C) had redirected

D) have redirected

6

In anticipation of Diwali, the Hindu Festival of Lights, families ________.

Which choice completes the text so that it conforms to the conventions of Standard English?

A) decorate their homes, purchase new clothes, and gifts are exchanged with loved ones

B) decorate their homes, they purchase new clothes, and their gifts are exchanged with loved ones

C) decorate their homes, purchase new clothes, and they exchange gifts with loved ones

D) decorate their homes, purchase new clothes, and exchange gifts with loved ones

7

In his seminal work The Origin of Species, Charles Darwin elucidates how species adapt to their environments, ________.

Which choice completes the text so that it conforms to the conventions of Standard English?

A) undergo evolutionary changes over time, and interacting with other organisms in complex ecological relationships

B) they are undergoing evolutionary changes over time, and interact with other organisms in complex ecological relationships

C) how they undergo evolutionary changes over time, and how they interact with other organisms in complex ecological relationships

D) undergo evolutionary changes over time, and how they interact with other organisms in complex ecological relationships

PRONOUN AGREEMENT

LESSON 1

An antecedent is a word or phrase that a pronoun refers to or replaces to avoid repetition.

EXAMPLE

- John went to the store, and he bought some groceries.

EXPLANATION *John* is the antecedent of *he*.

LESSON 2

To ensure clarity and avoid confusion, the pronoun must agree in number, gender, and person with its antecedent.

EXAMPLE

- The **people** on this island are known for **his** unique culture and traditions. (X)

- The **people** on this island are known for **their** unique culture and traditions. (O)

- **John** is known for **his** excellent leadership skills and ability to motivate **his students** toward achieving **their** goals. (O)

- The straying **cat** near my house hurt **its** paw and couldn't walk properly. (O)

LESSON 3 **Maintain a consistent point of view throughout your sentences.**

EXAMPLE

- If **we** want to lose weight, **you** should consider reducing your calorie intake and increasing your physical activity. (X)
- If **you** want to lose weight, **you** should consider reducing your calorie intake and increasing your physical activity. (O)

EXPLANATION Why should we consider that when YOU want to lose weight? It's YOU who should do that.

LESSON 4 **Confusing pronouns can occur when homophones (words that sound alike) are used incorrectly.**

There	It's an adverb.	There is a beautiful sunset over the ocean.
Their	It shows possession and is plural.	Scientists are using advanced technology to analyze their data and draw conclusions.
They're	It is a contraction for they are and replaces plural antecedent.	Since the bears are hungry, they're searching for berries in the forest.
Its	It is a possessive case and replaces a nonhuman singular noun.	The new car was so shiny that its paint reflected the sun.
It's	"It's" is a contraction for "it is" or "it has."	It's been a long day at work, but I'm looking forward to relaxing at home tonight.
Its'	It is not a valid word in the English language. Never pick this as an answer.	

LESSON 5

Pronoun case refers to the form a pronoun takes based on its function in a sentence: subjective, objective, or possessive. Use the correct pronoun case accordingly.

EXAMPLE 1

- **Me** and **my** brother are going to the beach. (X)
- My **brother** and **I** are going to the beach. (O)

EXPLANATION In this sentence, ***my brother and I*** are the subjects of the sentence, and therefore the subjective case pronoun I should be used instead of ***me***.

EXAMPLE 2

- Between **you** and **I**, there should be no secrets. (X)
- Between **you** and **me**, there should be no secrets. (O)

EXPLANATION In this sentence, ***you and me*** are the objects of the preposition ***between***; therefore, the objective case pronoun ***me*** should be used instead of ***I***.

LESSON 6

Ensure that pronouns agree in number with their antecedents.

EXAMPLE

- The **university** has decided to build a new dorm because **they** recently received a huge amount of donations. (X)
- The **university** has decided to build a new dorm because **it** recently received a huge amount of donations. (O)

EXPLANATION ***University*** is a singular noun and to replace a nonhuman singular antecedent, a singular pronoun ***it*** should be used instead of ***they***.

LESSON 7 **Do not confuse verbs with nouns when using pronouns.**

EXAMPLE

- Although the company CEO **promised** both to increase profits and not to lay off any staff, she failed to keep any of **them** after the shareholders' general meeting. (X)
- **Although the company CEO's promises** were both to cut taxes and improve services, she failed to keep any of **them** after the shareholders' general meeting. (O)

EXPLANATION The pronoun ***them*** replaces the noun ***promises***, not the verb ***promised***. Pronouns replace nouns, not verbs.

PRONOUN AGREEMENT PROBLEM SET

Answers are provided on page 210.

1

During _______ Hellenistic period, Greek civilization created stunning sculptures that depicted intricate details of the human form, which art historians are still studying and interpreting today.

Which choice completes the text so that it conforms to the conventions of Standard English?

A) its

B) its'

C) their

D) there

2

The United States must be able to balance _______ economic and political interests with moral and ethical responsibilities as a global leader.

Which choice completes the text so that it conforms to the conventions of Standard English?

A) it's

B) its

C) their

D) our

3

The study of literature not only exposes readers to different perspectives and ideas but also provides a valuable lens through which they can examine and appreciate _______ own cultural heritage.

Which choice completes the text so that it conforms to the conventions of Standard English?

A) they're

B) there

C) their

D) theirs

4

The principal of the school was deciding whether _______ or his brother would be the better candidate for the vacant teaching position.

Which choice completes the text so that it conforms to the conventions of Standard English?

A) he

B) him

C) he's

D) himself

5

A dolphin is a highly social marine mammal that thrives in oceans and seas around the world. With _______ sleek and streamlined body, the dolphin is well-adapted for swimming and navigating through the water with grace and agility.

Which choice completes the text so that it conforms to the conventions of Standard English?

A) their

B) its

C) her

D) they're

6

The restaurant advertised that _______ dishes were both healthy and delicious, but many customers found the food to be overly greasy and lacking in nutrients.

Which choice completes the text so that it conforms to the conventions of Standard English?

A) their

B) its

C) one's

D) your

7

The giant pandas (Ailuropoda melanoleuca) have a specialized diet that consists almost entirely of bamboo, which they eat for up to 14 hours a day. Despite their carnivorous ancestry, the pandas' digestive system has adapted to this plant-based diet, allowing _______ to extract the necessary nutrients from bamboo.

Which choice completes the text so that it conforms to the conventions of Standard English?

A) itself

B) it

C) them

D) one

8

Since ancient times, people in Japan have practiced the art of bonsai, the cultivation of miniature trees in containers. Bonsai trees are highly prized for _______ beauty and symbolism, and are often used to decorate homes, temples, and public spaces.

Which choice completes the text so that it conforms to the conventions of Standard English?

A) their

B) they're

C) its

D) it's

PRONOUN AGREEMENT PROBLEM SET

9

The use of chopsticks as eating utensils dates back to ancient China, where _______ initially used for cooking and only later adopted for use at the dining table.

Which choice completes the text so that it conforms to the conventions of Standard English?

A) it was

B) they were

C) you were

D) one was

10

For my teammate and _______ our performance on the field, we had to commit to practicing regularly and focusing on refining our skills instead of relying solely on natural talent.

Which choice completes the text so that it conforms to the conventions of Standard English?

A) I to improve

B) I were to improve

C) me to improve

D) me improve

11

When you want to provide video clips online, _______ ensure that the files are properly compressed and optimized for streaming in order to deliver a seamless viewing experience for your audience.

Which choice completes the text so that it conforms to the conventions of Standard English?

A) people need to

B) one needs to

C) it needs to

D) you need to

SUBJUNCTIVE MOOD

WHAT IS SUBJUNCTIVE MOOD

A verb form used to express various states of unreality or uncertainty, such as wishes, doubts, possibilities, and hypothetical situations. It is typically used in certain grammatical constructions and expressions of necessity, command, or recommendation.

There are two main types of subjunctive mood:

Present Subjunctive	Past Subjunctive

The present subjunctive is used to express hypothetical situations, doubts, wishes, emotions, and actions that are not yet completed. It is formed by using the base form of the verb, without adding -s or -es to the end, and is used in both singular and plural forms.

LESSON 1

After certain verbs or nouns that express demands, suggestions, or necessity, the subjunctive is used in the subordinate clause. The helping verb *should* can be omitted.

Verbs	advise decide demand desire insist move suggest urge command ask order recommend propose determine
Nouns	suggestion proposal recommendation argument

EXAMPLE

- My mom insisted that my brother ***should stop*** eating at night. (O)
- My mom insisted that my brother ***stop*** eating at night. (O)

EXPLANATION

****Be careful!**** When *should* is omitted, you might think there is a subject-verb disagreement in the sentence. Although the verb *'stop'* looks like a plural form and does not match the subject, it should stay as it is to be grammatically correct.

LESSON 2 **When using *it* as a placeholder in expressions of necessity or importance, the subjunctive is used in the clause following *that*. The helping verb *should* can be omitted.**

Rational	necessary important natural right wrong proper rational good imperative
Emotional	strange curious odd surprised regrettable fortunate a shame a pity

EXAMPLE 1 <u>Rational</u>

- It is essential that smoking ***will be banned***. (X)
- It is essential that smoking ***should be banned***. (O)
- It is essential that smoking ***be banned***. (O)

EXAMPLE 2 <u>Emotional</u>

- I am surprised that Alice ***should get*** a low grade on her term paper. (O)
- I am surprised that Alice ***get*** a low grade on her term paper. (X)

EXPLANATION After expressions of emotion, ***should*** is used in the subordinate clause. The base subjunctive without ***should*** is not used here.

Present Subjunctive	Past Subjunctive

The past subjunctive is used to express hypothetical or unreal situations in the present or past. It often appears in conditional sentences and uses specific verb forms.

LESSON 3 **Hypothetical situations expressing <u>the present</u>**
Structure: (If + subject + were / past tense verb, subject + would/could/might + base verb)

EXAMPLE

- If John ***was*** rich, he ***would*** not ***take*** the job. (X)
- If John ***were*** rich, he ***would*** not ***take*** the job. (O) (He is not rich so he will take the job.)
- If I ***had*** money, I would buy this car. (O) (I don't have money so I cannot buy this car.)

EXPLANATION When using the verb ***be***, use ***were*** for all subjects in the subjunctive mood to indicate a hypothetical situation.

LESSON 4

Hypothetical situations expressing <u>the past</u>.
Structure: (If + subject + had + past participle, subject + would/could/might + have + past participle)

EXAMPLE

- If John ***had*** eaten dinner, he ***might*** not ***have been*** so hungry at dinner last night. (I didn't eat dinner, so he was hungry last night.)
- If Mike ***had had*** extra five dollars, he ***could have bought*** a lottery ticket when he stopped by the convenience store. (Mike didn't have money, so he couldn't buy a lottery ticket.)

EXPLANATION

The first ***had*** is the auxiliary verb for the past perfect tense; the second ***had*** is the main verb meaning "possessed."

LESSON 5

<u>Past condition</u> affecting <u>the present</u>
Structure: (If + subject + had + past participle, subject + would/could/might + base verb)

EXAMPLE

- If I ***had married*** you ten years ago, our lives ***would be*** quite different now.

LESSON 6

Hypothetical future situations
Structure: (If + subject + were to / should + base verb, subject + would/will + base verb)

EXAMPLE

- If I ***were to win*** the lottery, I ***would donate*** a portion of the money to charity.
- If I ***should*** have more questions, I ***will call*** you.
- If you ***should have*** more questions, please ***do*** not ***hesitate*** to contact me.

EXPLANATION

Using ***should*** indicates a future possibility.

LESSON 7

You can invert the subject and auxiliary verb to form conditional sentences without "if."

EXAMPLE

- ***If*** I ***were*** to win the lottery, I would donate a portion of the money to charity.
- ***Were*** I to win the lottery, I would donate a portion of the money to charity.

- Please do not hesitate to contact me ***if*** you ***should have*** more questions.
- Please do not hesitate to contact me ***should*** you ***have*** more questions.

- ***If*** John ***had studied*** harder, he might have passed the exam yesterday.
  ➡ ***Had*** John ***studied*** harder, he might have passed the exam yesterday.
- John might have passed the exam yesterday ***if*** he ***had studied*** harder.
  ➡ John might have passed the exam yesterday ***had*** he ***studied*** harder.

EXPLANATION

While the more formal, inverted conditional structures may initially seem awkward or complex, they are frequently used in written English, especially in academic texts, literature, and formal correspondence.

LESSON 8

Don't confuse the subjunctive mood with the indicative mood. In the indicative mood, real and factual conditions are expressed using present tense verbs.

EXAMPLE

- If John wins the race, I **will buy** him a congratulatory drink at the bar.

EXPLANATION

This is a real possibility, not a hypothetical situation.

SUBJUNCTIVE MOOD PROBLEM SET

Answers are provided on page 211.

1

The HR manager recommended that after developing healthy cafeteria menus, _______ to promote healthy eating habits among employees.

Which choice completes the text so that it conforms to the conventions of Standard English?

A) wellness initiatives would also need to be implemented by the company

B) wellness initiatives also needed to be implemented by the company

C) the company also implement wellness initiatives

D) the company also implemented wellness initiatives

2

_______ more diligent in his studies, he could have achieved higher grades.

Which choice completes the text so that it conforms to the conventions of Standard English?

A) Had Joseph been

B) If Joseph would have been

C) If Joseph was

D) Were Joseph to be

3

Doctors advised that _______ for better outcomes.

Which choice completes the text so that it conforms to the conventions of Standard English?

A) a cancer patient make necessary lifestyle adjustments

B) a cancer patient made necessary lifestyle adjustments

C) necessary lifestyle adjustments would need to be made by a cancer patient

D) necessary lifestyle adjustments needed to be made by a cancer patient

4

If I were the president, I _______ education reform.

Which choice completes the text so that it conforms to the conventions of Standard English?

A) would prioritize

B) will prioritize

C) prioritized

D) would have prioritized

5

If _______ to my advice, they wouldn't be in this situation.

Which choice completes the text so that it conforms to the conventions of Standard English?

A) they would have listened

B) they listen

C) they had listened

D) they will listen

6

If _______ sunny tomorrow, we would go to the beach.

Which choice completes the text so that it conforms to the conventions of Standard English?

A) it is

B) it becomes

C) it will be

D) it should be

TRANSITIONS

WHAT IS TRANSITION

Transitions are words or phrases that help to connect ideas and guide the reader or listener from one thought to the next. They serve as a bridge between different ideas, sentences, or paragraphs, making the writing or speech smoother and easier to understand. Transitions can signal different relationships between ideas, such as cause and effect, comparison and contrast, or chronological order.

These are some transitional words that have been on the SAT.

Add Info.

- additionally
- furthermore
- moreover
- in addition
- Besides
- also

Cause and Effect

- accordingly
- as a result
- therefore
- thus
- for this reason
- to that end

Contrast

- alternately
- alternatively
- in contrast
- by contrast
- conversely
- however
- instead
- on the contrary
- on the other hand
- yet

Compare

- likewise
- similarly
- in comparison
- by the same token
- in the same manner
- meanwhile

Give Examples

- for example
- for instance
- specifically
- particularly

Concession

- nevertheless
- regardless
- still
- nonetheless
- even so
- despite
- in spite of
- that said

Sequence of Events

- afterward
- finally
- secondly
- subsequently
- ultimately
- consequently
- at the same time
- currently
- to begin with
- all the while
- next
- after all

Summary

- in short,
- in conclusion
- to conclude

Explain or Emphasize

- actually
- in fact
- indeed
- at any rate
- in other words
- namely

LESSON 1

Following are example sentences of each type of transition.

EXAMPLE

Add info	The school has implemented a new curriculum that focuses on project-based learning. ***In addition***, they have started offering more opportunities for students to participate in extracurricular activities.
Cause and Effect	The company has recently undergone significant restructuring to improve efficiency and reduce costs. ***Accordingly***, several departments have been merged and some positions have been eliminated.
Contrast	Many people enjoy listening to music while working or studying. ***Alternatively***, some may prefer to work or study in silence, avoiding any distractions that may interfere with their focus.
Compare	Many musicians are exploring new genres and experimenting with their sound. ***Similarly***, visual artists are also pushing boundaries and exploring new mediums.
Give Examples	There are many types of renewable energy, including solar, wind, hydro, and geothermal power. ***For example***, Germany has made great strides in utilizing solar energy, with over 50% of its electricity coming from solar panels on a sunny day.
Concession	The project faced several delays due to unforeseen circumstances. ***Nevertheless***, the team was able to complete it on time.
Sequence of Events	The company's stock price plummeted following the announcement of a major data breach. ***Afterward***, the CEO issued a statement to reassure customers and outline steps the company was taking to prevent future breaches.
Summary	I've been studying for weeks and taking practice exams, but I still don't feel prepared for the test. ***In short***, I need to review the material more thoroughly and create a better study plan.
Explain or Emphasize	The company's revenue has been steadily increasing over the past few years. ***Indeed***, it has nearly doubled since 2017.

LESSON 2

There are some unfamiliar words that you need to know.

EXAMPLE

Transition	Meaning	Example Sentence
To that end	To achieve that goal	I'm saving money to buy a house. ***To that end***, I've been working extra hours at my job."
Accordingly	Therefore	I have a project due tomorrow. ***Accordingly***, I need to work diligently tonight to ensure its completion.
By this token	For the similar reason	John has always been a hardworking student, consistently scoring high grades in his classes. ***By this token***, he was awarded a scholarship to pursue his dream of becoming a doctor.
After all	In the end	*** This transition is used when the expected outcome is different.** I thought the movie was going to be terrible, but ***after all***, it was quite enjoyable.
Namely	In other words	I have three favorite foods - pizza, sushi, and ice cream. ***Namely***, these are the foods that I could eat every day without getting tired of them.

LESSON 3

If you have trouble getting the transition questions right, don't look at the context that follows the transition. Try to make your own story using the transitions from the answer choices and jot down the story next to the choice.

EXAMPLE

The project faced several delays due to unforeseen circumstances. __________ the team was able to complete it on time.

A) **Rather**, huh?

B) **Nevertheless**, the project was finished on time.

C) Similarly, other projects in the company have experienced setbacks beyond their control.

D) For example, the supplier unexpectedly ran out of materials, and the project team had to find an alternative source.

EXPLANATION

"Rather" would not be an appropriate transition to use in this context. It is often used to introduce a contrast or an unexpected change of direction.

After you are done completing each answer choice, read the given context and select the one similar to yours.

TRANSITION PROBLEM SET

Answers are provided on page 212.

1

The company's stock price plummeted following the announcement of a major data breach. ________ the CEO issued a statement to reassure customers and outline steps the company was taking to prevent future breaches.

Which choice completes the text with the most logical transition?

A) Afterward,

B) In contrast,

C) Particularly,

D) To that end,

2

In the mid-21st century, advances in quantum computing significantly accelerated the pace of scientific research. Complex calculations that used to take months could now be solved in a matter of seconds. ________, scientists were able to make groundbreaking discoveries at an unprecedented rate.

Which choice completes the text with the most logical transition?

A) At the same time,

B) As a result,

C) Similarly

D) Instead,

3

In the early 20th century, as the women's suffrage movement gained momentum in the United States, different regions adopted unique methods to promote the cause. In New York, the Women's Suffrage Association organized large parades and rallies to draw public attention. _____ in Chicago, prominent figures like Jane Addams gave powerful speeches at major events, emphasizing the importance of women's voting rights.

Which choice completes the text with the most logical transition?

A) For instance,

B) Nevertheless,

C) Similarly,

D) On the contrary,

4

When faced with a difficult decision, some people prefer to weigh the pros and cons before making a choice. ________ others may go with their gut instinct, following their intuition and emotions.

Which choice completes the text with the most logical transition?

A) Alternatively,

B) Subsequently,

C) Accordingly,

D) Furthermore,

Answers are provided on page 212~213.

5

The team struggled to find a breakthrough in their research, but after conducting further experiments and analyzing the data, they made an important discovery. ________ they published their findings in a scientific journal.

Which choice completes the text with the most logical transition?

A) Instead,

B) Similarly,

C) Afterward,

D) Conversely,

6

Virtual meetings can save time and money compared to in-person meetings. ________ they can also lack the personal connection and nonverbal cues of face-to-face interactions.

Which choice completes the text with the most logical transition?

A) As a result,

B) Particularly,

C) To that end,

D) By the same token,

7

Online shopping has become increasingly popular in recent years, with more and more consumers turning to e-commerce sites for convenience and variety. ________ retailers are investing in new technologies not only to attract online users to their sites but also to enhance the online shopping experience, such as virtual try-ons and personalized recommendations.

Which choice completes the text with the most logical transition?

A) Instead,

B) Similarly,

C) Particularly,

D) Accordingly,

8

The film director spent years developing his script and scouting locations before filming began. ________ after a long and arduous process, the movie premiered to rave reviews and earned multiple awards.

Which choice completes the text with the most logical transition?

A) Finally,

B) To that end,

C) Conversely,

D) In addition,

TRANSITION PROBLEM SET

Answers are provided on page 213.

9

Many countries build renewable energy infrastructure to reduce their dependence on fossil fuels. ________ Germany has made great strides in utilizing solar energy, with over 50% of its electricity coming from solar panels on a sunny day.

Which choice completes the text with the most logical transition?

A) For example,

B) Similarly,

C) On the other hand,

D) Still,

10

Recent studies have highlighted the positive effects of physical exercise on mental health. Regular physical activity can decrease symptoms of depression and anxiety. ________, it also contributes to overall physical well-being, strengthening the heart, improving lung capacity, and enhancing muscle function.

Which choice completes the text with the most logical transition?

A) In contrast,

B) For instance,

C) In addition,

D) Similarly,

11

With the rise of remote work and online learning, traditional office and classroom environments are becoming less common. ________ companies and universities are exploring innovative ways to foster collaboration and engagement among virtual teams and students.

Which choice completes the text with the most logical transition?

A) At the same time,

B) Increasingly,

C) Particularly,

D) Conversely,

12

The company's revenue has been steadily increasing over the past few years. ________ it has nearly doubled since 2017.

Which choice completes the text with the most logical transition?

A) Indeed,

B) Furthermore,

C) Instead,

D) At the same time,

Answers are provided on page 213~214.

13

The city has seen a significant increase in bike ridership over the past few years. ________ local officials have started to invest in more bike lanes and infrastructure to support this mode of transportation.

Which choice completes the text with the most logical transition?

A) At the same time,

B) Therefore,

C) In contrast,

D) Instead,

14

Critics have dubbed Christopher Nolan the "master of mind-bending cinema," a title that has been used to describe his films' complex narratives and non-linear structures. ________ Nolan has expressed discomfort with the label, saying in interviews that he doesn't set out to confuse audiences and that he simply tells stories in the way that he finds most interesting.

Which choice completes the text with the most logical transition?

A) However,

B) Similarly,

C) As a result,

D) Indeed,

15

We've set up a scholarship fund to help students from low-income families. ________ we're organizing a fundraising event next month.".

Which choice completes the text with the most logical transition?

A) Also,

B) Instead,

C) To that end,

D) In addition,

16

Many people have switched to online shopping during the pandemic to avoid going to physical stores. ________ some prefer the traditional shopping experience.

Which choice completes the text with the most logical transition?

A) Still,

B) Finally,

C) As a result,

D) In addition,

TRANSITION PROBLEM SET

Answers are provided on page 214.

17

Historians have called Marie Curie the "mother of modern physics," a title that recognizes her groundbreaking work on radioactivity and the discovery of two new elements. ________ some scientists argue that the nickname is problematic because it reinforces the idea that women in science are only valuable as mothers and nurturers. Instead, they suggest calling Curie a "pioneer" or "innovator" in her field.

Which choice completes the text with the most logical transition?

A) Finally,

B) However,

C) At any rate,

D) Also,

18

The CEO of the company had promised to increase salaries and benefits for all employees, but the board of directors vetoed the proposal. ________ the CEO continued to advocate for the well-being of the workers and implemented other measures to improve their quality of life.

Which choice completes the text with the most logical transition?

A) As a result,

B) Nevertheless,

C) In addition,

D) Likewise,

19

On the one hand, studying abroad can be a life-changing experience for young adults. They get to immerse themselves in a new culture, learn a new language, and gain valuable international experience. ________ studying abroad can also be very expensive and logistically challenging, especially for students who come from low-income families or who have other responsibilities back home.

Which choice completes the text with the most logical transition?

A) On the other hand,

B) As a result,

C) Similarly,

D) Finally,

20

I have three favorite foods - pizza, sushi, and ice cream. ________ these are the foods that I could eat every day without getting tired of them."

Which choice completes the text with the most logical transition?

A) Namely,

B) Finally,

C) Instead,

D) Accordingly,

TRANSITION PROBLEM SET

Answers are provided on page 214~215.

21

The athlete suffered a minor injury during training. ________ she went on to win the competition and set a new personal record.

Which choice completes the text with the most logical transition?

A) Nevertheless,

B) At the same time,

C) Particularly,

D) For example,

22

Advances in technology have revolutionized many industries, including healthcare, transportation, and entertainment. ________ self-driving cars are being developed by companies like Tesla and Google, which could change the way we commute and travel in the future.

Which choice completes the text with the most logical transition?

A) Accordingly,

B) Instead,

C) Even so,

D) For example,

23

I was planning to go to the beach this weekend; ________ the weather forecast is predicting thunderstorms.

Which choice completes the text with the most logical transition?

A) as a result,

B) however,

C) finally,

D) in addition,

24

Historian John Smith explains why a particular medieval castle was likely built for defensive purposes. First, the castle's strategic location on a hilltop overlooking a nearby river would have made it an ideal defensive stronghold. ________ the castle's thick stone walls and fortified towers suggest that it was designed to withstand a prolonged siege.

Which choice completes the text with the most logical transition?

A) Particularly,

B) Second,

C) For example,

D) Thus,

25

In the 4th century BCE, Aristotle classified living organisms based on observable characteristics, a system that appears simplistic by today's standards. _______, modern biological classifications, built on genetic analysis and complex data, often align surprisingly well with Aristotle's original groupings, suggesting his insights were remarkably perceptive.

Which choice completes the text with the most logical transition?

A) For example,

B) That said,

C) Therefore,

D) In conclusion,

DANGLING MODIFIERS

WHAT IS DANGLING MODIFIERS

Dangling modifiers are phrases or clauses that do not clearly and logically modify a word or phrase in the sentence. They are called "dangling" because they are not attached to the correct word or phrase in the sentence and can create confusion or ambiguity for the reader.

LESSON 1

A dangling participle occurs when a participle (a verb form that typically ends in "-ing" or "-ed") is placed at the beginning or end of a sentence and is not properly connected to the subject of the sentence, leading to unclear or illogical meaning. (For more information, go back to the Participle chapter. pg.59)

EXAMPLE 1

- Defeating 133 large invaders' battleships with only 12 ships, remarkable strategic prowess and naval leadership were demonstrated by Admiral Yi Sun-shin. (X)
- Defeating 133 large invaders' battleships with only 12 ships, Admiral Yi Sun-shin demonstrated remarkable strategic prowess and naval leadership. (O)

EXPLANATION

The participial phrase ***Defeating 133 large invaders' battleships with only 12 ships*** should modify ***Admiral Yi Sun-shin***, not ***remarkable strategic prowess and naval leadership***. The subject performing the action is ***Admiral Yi Sun-shin***.

EXAMPLE 2

- Using a combination of herbs and spices, the flavor was added to the dish and impressed the guests at the dinner party. (X)
- Using a combination of herbs and spices, the chef added flavor to the dish and impressed the guests at the dinner party. (O)

EXPLANATION

The participial phrase ***Using a combination of herbs and spices*** should modify ***the chef***, who performed the action, not ***the flavor***.

EXAMPLE 3

- After discovering ancient seeds in a remote cave in China, the proposal by botanist Dr. Choi claims that early human diets were more diverse than previously thought. (X)
- After discovering ancient seeds in a remote cave in China, botanist Dr. Choi has proposed that early human diets were more diverse than previously thought. (O)

EXPLANATION The participial phrase ***After discovering ancient seeds in a remote cave in China*** should modify ***botanist Dr. Choi***, not ***the proposal***. Dr. Choi is the one who discovered the seeds.

LESSON 2 **Modifiers tend to modify the word that is closest to them in the sentence.**

EXAMPLE 1

- ***Upon receiving an inheritance from his rich father***, a significant portion was donated to charity by John. (X)
- ***Upon receiving an inheritance from his rich father***, John donated a significant portion to charity. (O)

EXPLANATION The prepositional phrase ***Upon receiving an inheritance from his billionaire father*** should logically modify ***John***, not ***a significant portion***. Placing ***John*** immediately after the modifier clarifies the sentence.

EXAMPLE 2

- The board of directors has decided to build a new wing ***during the weekly meeting***. (X)
- ***During the weekly meeting***, the board of directors has decided to build a new wing. (O)

EXPLANATION *During the weekly meeting* is a prepositional phrase that acts as an adverb modifying when the action will occur. And there are two actions – decided and build. Is it possible to build a new wing(building) during the meeting? How long would the meeting take to finish the project? Therefore, *During the weekly meeting* should modify the verb *decided* to make sense. Thus, you need to place the phrase in front of a sentence so that it can be closer to *decide* than *build*.

LESSON 3

Avoid placing a modifier between a participial phrase and an independent clause if it creates ambiguity.

EXAMPLE 1

- Aided by advanced technology, ***including*** machine learning algorithms and artificial intelligence, the self-driving car navigates through traffic without any human intervention. (X)

- Aided by advanced technology, ***which includes*** machine learning algorithms and artificial intelligence, the self-driving car navigates through traffic without any human intervention. (O)

EXPLANATION If a participial phrase is used in between another participial phrase and an independent clause, you don't know whether that phrase modifies the preceding noun or the subject of the main clause. However, inserting "which" or "that" can clarify the ambiguity because it tells that the relative clause modifies the preceding noun.

DANGLING MODIFIER PROBLEM SET

Answers are provided on page 216.

1

Since discovering a fossilized jawbone in Ethiopia, ________ may have evolved much earlier than previously thought.

Which choice completes the text so that it conforms to the conventions of Standard English?

A) scientists have argued that early humans

B) scientists' argument is that early humans

C) early humans, scientists have argued,

D) the argument scientists have made is that early humans

2

Encouraged by one of her professors, ________to gain more experience in her field of study.

Which choice completes the text so that it conforms to the conventions of Standard English?

A) Jane decided to apply for a summer internship at a research laboratory

B) an application was sent for a summer internship at a research laboratory for Jane

C) a summer internship at a research laboratory was applied by Jane

D) an application sent by Jane was for a summer internship at a research laboratory

3

Known to be highly venomous, ________ by using its powerful venom to paralyze and kill its prey.

Which choice completes the text so that it conforms to the conventions of Standard English?

A) the blue-ringed octopus's hunting targets crustaceans

B) crustaceans are hunted by the blue-ring octopus

C) Hunting crustaceans is acted by the blue-ringed octopus

D) the blue-ringed octopus hunts crustaceans

4

Through offering a reasonable salary, ________ are motivated to perform well and contribute to the growth and success of the organization.

Which choice completes the text so that it conforms to the conventions of Standard English?

A) skilled employees–attracted and retained by companies–

B) companies' attraction and retention of skilled employees can be achieved: they

C) companies can attract and retain skilled employees who

D) attracting and retaining skilled employees can be done by companies, and they

DANGLING MODIFIER PROBLEM SET

5

By disclosing his recent transaction, ________ to his competitors and jeopardized his company's negotiating position.

Which choice completes the text so that it conforms to the conventions of Standard English?

A) John's revelation of sensitive information is advertently done

B) John inadvertently revealed sensitive information

C) sensitive information was inadvertently revealed by John

D) inadvertently revealing sensitive information is done by John

6

By mixing Mentos and Coke, ________ a fountain of soda high into the air, demonstrating a popular science experiment.

Which choice completes the text so that it conforms to the conventions of Standard English?

A) Lucy's explosive reaction shot

B) an explosive reaction occurred, shooting

C) Lucy created an explosive reaction that shot

D) an explosion created by Lucy reacted in a way that

7

As a representative from several environmental organizations, ________ the possibility of collaborating on a project to promote sustainable practices and reduce waste in their local community.

Which choice completes the text so that it conforms to the conventions of Standard English?

A) Skyler discussed with Alice

B) Skyler and Alice discussed

C) Skyler, who discussed with Alice

D) Skyler and Alice, they discussed

BOUNDARIES

WHAT IS BOUNDARIES

Boundary questions deal with the connection between phrases, clauses, and sentences.

LESSON 1 **Some transitional adverbs can be placed at the beginning, in the middle, or at the end of a clause without changing the meaning.**

EXAMPLE 1

- I really want to go to the party tonight; **however**, I have an important exam tomorrow and need to study. I'm disappointed that I won't be able to see my friends. (O)

- I really want to go to the party tonight; I, **however**, have an important exam tomorrow and need to study. I'm disappointed that I won't be able to see my friends. (O)

- I really want to go to the party tonight; I have an important exam tomorrow and need to study, **however**. I'm disappointed that I won't be able to see my friends. (O)

- I really want to go to the party tonight. I have an important exam tomorrow and need to study, **however**; I'm disappointed that I won't be able to see my friends. (O)

EXPLANATION The placement of "however" does not alter the relationship between the clauses. It still contrasts the desire to go to the party with the need to study.

EXAMPLE 2

- I really want to go to the party tonight, **however**; I have an important exam tomorrow and need to study. I'm disappointed that I won't be able to see my friends. (X)
- Ben does not look happy about it, **rather**; he seems quite upset. (X)
- Ben does not look happy about it; **rather**, he seems quite upset. (O)

EXPLANATION Conjunctive adverbs are used to connect two independent clauses together. More specifically, they join the idea of preceding clauses.

EXAMPLE 3

- I really want to go to the party tonight; I have an important exam tomorrow and need to study. **However**, I'm disappointed that I won't be able to see my friends. (X)

EXPLANATION There is no contrasting idea between the preceding clause and the last sentence.

LESSON 2 **There is one adverb that the SAT uses only at the end of the clause: though.**

EXAMPLE

I'm not a big fan of Korean food, but I decided to try the Galbi dish anyway. It turned out to be _______ I was surprised by how much I enjoyed it.

A) delicious, though:
B) delicious, though,
C) delicious. Though:
D) delicious though

EXPLANATION Try to pick ", though;" or ", though:" or ", though." because this would most likely be the answer. The answer is A.

LESSON 3

You need to parse the complex sentence to understand its structure. In other words, Understand the structure of complex sentences by identifying clauses and modifiers.

EXAMPLE

Galileo Galilei is perhaps best known for inventing the early microscope and observing planets and stars, but he also dedicated himself to physics, the study of motion and __________ that the speed of fall of a heavy object is not proportional to its weight.

A) force; demonstrating
B) force. Demonstrating
C) force demonstrating
D) force, demonstrating

EXPLANATION

The first clause (*Galileo Galilei is perhaps best known for inventing the early microscope and observing planets and stars)* is joined by a coordinating conjunction with a comma *(, but)*. And then there is the second independent clause (*he also dedicated himself to physics*) and a comma (,). Then there is a noun phrase and a conjunction. (*the study of motion and* ___)

By looking at the answer choices, you notice there are punctuations after force. Now by reading the context, you should see the phrase (*the study of motion and force*) is an appositive defining physics.

Next, you need to check whether (*demonstrating that the speed of fall of a heavy object is not proportional to its weight.*) is a clause. Since demonstrating is a progressive form without a be verb, it is either a gerund or participle, and (*that the speed of fall of a heavy object is not proportional to its weight.*) clause is an object of demonstrating. Thus, it is not a clause so the answer choices A and B are eliminated. Now, you need to see if demonstrating modifies the *force* or the subject. You can easily tell it modifies the subject and needs a comma. The answer is D.

LESSON 4

A parenthetical clause is inserted when it is relatively less important than rest of the clause in a sentence.

EXAMPLE 1

- Michelle has an excuse, and ***many believe that*** it was nothing more than a feeble attempt to avoid taking responsibility for her actions. (O)
- Michelle has an excuse that ***many believe*** was nothing more than a feeble attempt to avoid taking responsibility for her actions. (O)

EXPLANATION The clause *many believe* can become a modifier as seen in the second example sentence.

EXAMPLE 2

- In the middle of the ancient forest stood a towering oak tree, a sight **that many believe** inspires awe - a natural landmark where locals, if seeking solace, would often find themselves. (X)
- In the middle of the ancient forest stood a towering oak tree, a sight **many believe inspiring** awe - a natural landmark where locals, if seeking solace, would often find themselves. (O)

EXPLANATION This is an inverted sentence in which the verb is *stood* and the subject is *oak tree*. Without a conjunction, there cannot be another clause in the sentence. By using the adjective *inspiring*, the later group of words becomes an appositive phrase.

EXAMPLE 3

- **Scientists believe that** if this zero-gravity rock were to be analyzed, it could provide valuable insights into the composition and formation of celestial bodies in space.
- If this zero-gravity rock were to be analyzed, **scientists believe**, it could provide valuable insights into the composition and formation of celestial bodies in space.

EXPLANATION The parenthetical clause can be in between the subordinate and main clause.

LESSON 5

Appositive phrases or modifiers can follow one another to add layers of description.

EXAMPLE

In his examination of Charles Dickens' novel, Great Expectations, literary critic James Peterson notes that the book portrays the societal divisions of Victorian England as "entrenched in rigid class structures," ***a fitting observation*** considering the setting of the novel in a time characterized by social stratification and economic disparities, ***a stark contrast*** that highlights the vast differences in living conditions, opportunities, and privileges between the upper and lower classes.

EXPLANATION

The multiple appositive phrases provide detailed commentary on the subject, each modifying a different noun.

LESSON 6

Identify where a modifying phrase ends to maintain sentence clarity.

EXAMPLE

- I made a student ID card—the purple plastic card with my name, photograph, and student identification number on it to gain access to the university's facilities and resources. (X)
- I made a student ID card—the purple plastic card with my name, photograph, and student identification number on it—to gain access to the university's facilities and resources. (O)

EXPLANATION

The phrase ***to gain access to the university's facilities and resources*** explains **why** the card was made, not a description of the card itself. Placing the phrase outside the description clarifies the sentence.

BOUNDARIES PROBLEM SET

Answers are provided on page 216.

1

The invention of the Post-it Note can be traced back to a 3M scientist named Spencer Silver, who created a low-tack, reusable adhesive in the late ________ it wasn't until several years later that a colleague named Art Fry realized the adhesive's potential as a bookmark.

Which choice completes the text so that it conforms to the conventions of Standard English?

A) 1960s. However,

B) 1960s, however,

C) 1960s, however

D) 1960s however

2

Some math experts argue that Albert Einstein's theories are merely the result of mathematical ________ to perceive and understand mathematical concepts, which can be honed through practice and study.

Which choice completes the text so that it conforms to the conventions of Standard English?

A) intuition. A natural ability,

B) intuition. A natural ability

C) intuition, a natural ability,

D) intuition, a natural ability

3

Throughout history, people in many cultures have used herbal remedies to treat common ailments such as headaches, indigestion, and ________ modern medicine has largely replaced the use of herbs in clinical settings, herbal remedies continue to be a popular choice for people seeking natural alternatives to pharmaceutical drugs.

Which choice completes the text so that it conforms to the conventions of Standard English?

A) colds. While

B) colds, while

C) colds while

D) colds and while

4

The intricate interplay between genetic predisposition, environmental factors, and lifestyle choices, which can significantly impact an individual's risk of developing chronic diseases, underscores the complexity of modern ________ the importance of personalized medicine.

Which choice completes the text so that it conforms to the conventions of Standard English?

A) healthcare. Highlights

B) healthcare, and highlights

C) healthcare and highlights

D) healthcare; highlights

Answers are provided on page 216~217.

5

The ancient Egyptians believed that the heart was the center of a person's being and held their ________ so during mummification, the heart was left in the body while other organs were removed and placed in canopic jars for safekeeping in the afterlife.

Which choice completes the text so that it conforms to the conventions of Standard English?

A) emotions and intellect,

B) emotions; intellect

C) emotions, and intellect

D) emotions, and intellect,

6

In his early works, Spanish artist Pablo Picasso was heavily influenced by the styles of other artists, such as the Blue Period inspired by the somber works of El ________ Rose Period influenced by the brighter, more colorful style of Henri Matisse.

Which choice completes the text so that it conforms to the conventions of Standard English?

A) Greco, and the

B) Greco and the

C) Greco. The

D) Greco, the

7

The sea otter (Enhydra lutris) is a playful and intelligent marine mammal that is found along the coasts of the North Pacific Ocean. Sea otters are unique among marine mammals in that they do not have a layer of blubber to keep them ________ they rely on their thick, waterproof fur to stay dry and insulated.

Which choice completes the text so that it conforms to the conventions of Standard English?

A) warm, instead,

B) warm, instead;

C) warm, instead

D) warm; instead,

8

The humpback whale (Megaptera novaeangliae) is a massive marine mammal that is known for its complex and haunting ________ whales use these songs to communicate with one another during their migrations, which can cover distances of up to 16,000 miles (25,750 kilometers) each year.

Which choice completes the text so that it conforms to the conventions of Standard English?

A) songs, humpback

B) songs and humpback

C) songs humpback

D) songs. Humpback

Answers are provided on page 217.

9

Across many cultures and throughout history, people have used dance as a form of expression, celebration, and social interaction. From traditional folk dances to modern styles such as hip-hop and ________ continues to be a vibrant and dynamic art form that brings people together.

Which choice completes the text so that it conforms to the conventions of Standard English?

A) salsa, dance,

B) salsa dance

C) salsa, dance

D) salsa. Dance

10

Throughout history, people in many cultures have used meditation as a means of achieving inner peace, spiritual enlightenment, and physical health. Today, meditation is a popular practice in many parts of the world, with many scientific ________ its potential benefits for reducing stress, improving mental clarity, and promoting well-being.

Which choice completes the text so that it conforms to the conventions of Standard English?

A) studies, showing

B) studies. Showing

C) studies showing

D) studies, and showing

11

For millennia, people in the Middle East have used henna to dye their hair and decorate their bodies for special occasions. Henna is made from the leaves of the henna ________ are ground into a powder and mixed with water to form a paste that can be applied to the skin or hair.

Which choice completes the text so that it conforms to the conventions of Standard English?

A) plant, which

B) plant,

C) plant and

D) plant, and

12

Since ancient times, people in Japan have practiced the art of bonsai, the cultivation of miniature trees in ________ trees are highly prized for their beauty and symbolism and are often used to decorate homes, temples, and public spaces.

Which choice completes the text so that it conforms to the conventions of Standard English?

A) containers. Bonsai

B) containers and Bonsai

C) containers, Bonsai

D) containers Bonsai

Answers are provided on page 217.

13

The Golden Gate Bridge is an iconic landmark in ________ the Golden Gate Strait, connecting the city to Marin County.

Which choice completes the text so that it conforms to the conventions of Standard English?

A) California, located in the city of San Francisco, it spans

B) California; located in the city of San Francisco, it spans

C) California and is located in the city of San Francisco, it spans

D) California; located in the city of San Francisco, spanning

14

The museum's latest exhibit featured a stunning collection of ancient artifacts, drawing visitors from around the world. Some of the most fascinating objects in the exhibit were not the most visually ________ the curator explained that these unassuming pieces often had the most intriguing stories and historical significance.

Which choice completes the text so that it conforms to the conventions of Standard English?

A) impressive, though:

B) impressive, though,

C) impressive. Though,

D) impressive though

RHETORICAL SYNTHESIS

WHAT IS RHETORICAL SYNTHESIS

Rhetorical synthesis questions provide a set of bullet points containing related information on a topic. The task is to select the option that best uses relevant information to achieve a specific goal.

EXAMPLE QUESTION

While researching a topic, a student has taken the following notes:

- Isambard Kingdom Brunel (1806–1859) was a British civil engineer.
- He designed the Clifton Suspension Bridge over the Avon Gorge in Bristol, England.
- The bridge has a span of 702 feet (214 meters) and a height of 245 feet (75 meters) above the river.
- Its construction began in 1831 but was not completed until 1864, after Brunel's death.
- The bridge features two iconic stone towers and wrought iron chains supporting the deck.

The student wants to describe the Clifton Suspension Bridge to an audience unfamiliar with Isambard Kingdom Brunel. Which choice most effectively uses relevant information from the notes to accomplish this goal?

A) The Clifton Suspension Bridge, designed by British civil engineer Isambard Kingdom Brunel, spans 702 feet over the Avon Gorge in Bristol, England.

B) Spanning 702 feet over the Avon Gorge, the Clifton Suspension Bridge was designed by Isambard Kingdom Brunel but wasn't completed until after his death.

C) Isambard Kingdom Brunel began constructing the Clifton Suspension Bridge in 1831, but it was not finished until 1864.

D) The Clifton Suspension Bridge is a remarkable structure in Bristol, England, that features stone towers and iron chains.

BUILDING STANDARD SOLVING SKILLS

STEP 1

Don't read the bullet points first. Go directly to the question that says "The student wants to~" and identify the goal.

Understand the Specific Goal:

- Identify What Is Being Asked: Read the question carefully to determine exactly what the student wants to achieve (e.g., emphasizing a duration, providing a specific example, comparing two items).
- Determine the Required Focus: Understand whether the goal is to highlight a similarity, a difference, a specific detail, or to set up a broader discussion.

STEP 2

Carefully read the notes and match the points to the goal:

EXAMPLE 1

- Key Information to Include:
  - The bridge's name: Clifton Suspension Bridge.
  - Location: Over the Avon Gorge in Bristol, England.
  - Designer: Isambard Kingdom Brunel, a British civil engineer.
  - Notable features: Span of 702 feet, stone towers, wrought iron chains.
- Less Emphasis on:
  - Detailed history of construction dates.
  - Brunel's death and the bridge's completion after his death (unless directly relevant).

STEP 3

Evaluate Each Choice:

- Option A:
  - Introduces the bridge and mentions Brunel as a British civil engineer.
  - Provides the bridge's span and location.
  - Focuses on describing the bridge to an audience unfamiliar with Brunel, offering necessary context about who he is.
- Option B:
  - Starts with the bridge's span and location.
  - Mentions Brunel but adds the detail that the bridge wasn't completed until after his death.
  - The information about the bridge's completion after his death may not be essential for a basic description.

- Option C:
  - Focuses on Brunel's involvement and construction dates.
  - Does not provide descriptive details about the bridge itself.
  - May not effectively describe the bridge to someone unfamiliar with Brunel.
- Option D:
  - Describes the bridge's features: stone towers and iron chains.
  - Does not mention Brunel at all.
  - While it describes the bridge, it omits the designer.

STEP 4

Eliminate Incorrect or Less Effective Options:

- Option B: Includes less relevant detail about the bridge's completion after Brunel's death, which might not be essential for the audience.
- Option C: Focuses too much on Brunel and construction dates, lacking descriptive details of the bridge.
- Option D: Omits Brunel entirely, ***which might be acceptable if the question specified an audience familiar with Isambard Kingdom Brunel.***

STEP 5

Select the Best Choice:

- Option A is the most effective. It introduces the bridge, provides key details about its design and location, and briefly introduces Brunel as a British civil engineer, which is helpful for an audience unfamiliar with him.

Efficient Tactic for Solving Rhetorical Synthesis Questions "Without Referring to the Notes":

To save time for other questions, use this strategy for "rhetorical synthesis" questions: focus exclusively on the question stem and answer choices, without referring to notes.

STEP 1 **Read the Question Stem Carefully:**

- Identify the Specific Goal:
  - Look for action verbs and keywords such as "emphasize," "specify," "contrast," "similarity," "difference," "explain," "role," etc.
  - Understand exactly what the question is asking you to find or highlight.

- Determine the Focus:
  - Is the question asking for a similarity or a difference?
  - Is it asking you to explain, specify, or provide an example?

STEP 2 **Analyze the Answer Choices:**

- Look for Keywords Matching the Goal:
  - Scan each answer choice for words or phrases that align with the goal identified in the question stem.

- Eliminate Irrelevant or Incorrect Options:
  - Discard choices that do not address the goal.
  - Remove options that focus on different aspects or introduce unrelated information.

- Compare Remaining Choices:
  - Consider which choice most directly and effectively achieves the goal.

STEP 3 **Use Logical Reasoning:**

- Assess How Each Choice Aligns with the Goal:
  - Does the choice emphasize what the question wants?
  - Is it focusing on the correct elements (e.g., similarity, difference, specific detail)?

- Beware of Distractors:
  - Be cautious of choices that partially address the goal but introduce contradictions or irrelevant details.

STEP 4 **Select the Best Answer:**

- Choose the Option That Best Fulfills the Goal:
  - The correct choice should clearly and directly accomplish what is asked.

EXAMPLE QUESTION

While researching a topic, a student has taken the following notes:

- In 2023, a group of educational researchers developed a new study technique called "Active Recall Mapping."
- This technique involves students creating mind maps while actively recalling information from their lectures and readings.
- The mind maps allow students to visualize connections between concepts and improve their understanding.
- Students reported that this method helped them retain information better compared to traditional note-taking.
- The technique became popular because it encouraged deeper engagement with the material.

The student wants to explain an advantage of the "Active Recall Mapping" study technique. Which choice most effectively uses relevant information from the notes to accomplish this goal?

A) "Active Recall Mapping" involves students creating mind maps while recalling information from their lectures and readings.

B) Students reported that using mind maps helped them retain information better than traditional note-taking.

C) The "Active Recall Mapping" technique became popular because it encouraged deeper engagement with the material.

D) In 2023, educational researchers developed the "Active Recall Mapping" technique to help students study more effectively.

APPLYING THE STRATEGY

STEP 1 **Read the Question Stem Carefully:**

- Identify the Specific Goal:
  - The student wants to explain an advantage of the "Active Recall Mapping" study technique.
- Determine the Focus:
  - The question asks for a choice that **most effectively uses relevant information from the notes to explain an advantage of the technique.**

STEP 2 **Analyze the Answer Choices:**

Choice A

- **Content**: "Active Recall Mapping" involves students creating mind maps while recalling information from their lectures and readings.
- **Analysis**: This choice describes the process of the technique but does not explain why it is advantageous. It focuses on what the technique involves, not why it is advantageous.

Choice B

- **Content**: Students reported that using mind maps helped them retain information better than traditional note-taking.
- **Analysis**: This choice mentions an advantage: improved retention compared to traditional note-taking. However, it references using mind maps in general, not specifically the "Active Recall Mapping" technique. It doesn't directly connect the advantage to Active Recall Mapping, which is the focus.

Choice C

- **Content**: The "Active Recall Mapping" technique became popular because it encouraged deeper engagement with the material.
- **Analysis:**This choice directly states an advantage of Active Recall Mapping: it encourages deeper engagement with the material.

<u>It aligns with the notes:</u> *"The technique became popular because it encouraged deeper engagement with the material."* It effectively uses relevant information to explain an advantage of the technique.

Choice D

- **Content**: In 2023, educational researchers developed the "Active Recall Mapping" technique to help students study more effectively.
- **Analysis**: This choice provides background information about the development of the technique.It mentions the intended purpose but does not explain a specific advantage. It lacks details on how it helps students study more effectively.

STEP 3

Use Logical Reasoning:

- Assess Alignment with the Goal:
  - Choice C best fulfills the goal by explaining an advantage of the technique and directly referencing Active Recall Mapping.

- Beware of Distractors:
  - Choice B mentions an advantage but does not explicitly connect it to Active Recall Mapping, making it less effective.
  - Choices A and D do not focus on explaining an advantage.

STEP 4

Select the Best Answer:

- Choice C is the most effective because it:
  - Directly explains an advantage of the "Active Recall Mapping" technique.
  - Uses relevant information from the notes.
  - Aligns with the goal of the question.

NOTE BOX

Be careful! Always review all answer choices thoroughly, even if one initially seems correct. If two choices appear plausible, refer to the student's notes for clarification. Often, the latter choice aligns better with the notes or the question's intent. See the example question on the next page for guidance.

EXAMPLE QUESTION

While researching a topic, a student has taken the following notes:

- An ocean's rainfall in the surrounding region contributes freshwater, reducing its salinity.
- An ocean's evaporation in the surrounding region removes water, increasing its salinity.
- The ocean's saltiness, or salinity, is the measure of the concentration of dissolved salts in seawater, typically expressed in parts per thousand (ppt).
- Oceans with high evaporation and low rainfall typically have salinity levels above 35 ppt, while oceans with high rainfall and low evaporation usually have salinity levels below 35 ppt.
- The Atlantic Ocean has high salinity.
- The Pacific Ocean has low salinity.

The student wants to compare the saltiness of two oceans. Which choice most effectively uses relevant information from the notes to accomplish this goal?

A) The high-salinity Pacific Ocean is saltier than the low-salinity Atlantic Ocean.

B) By comparing the rainfall and evaporation levels of the Atlantic and Pacific oceans, one can determine their relative saltiness, or salinity.

C) In both the Atlantic and the Pacific Oceans, saltiness is determined by the balance of evaporation and rainfall in the region.

D) The Atlantic Ocean's measure of the concentration of dissolved salts in seawater, also known as salinity, is greater than the Pacific Ocean.

EXPLANATION

Choice A initially seems correct without referencing the notes, as it provides a direct comparison. However, it is incorrect because it inaccurately describes the Pacific Ocean as having high salinity.

The notes clearly state that the Pacific Ocean has low salinity, while the Atlantic has high salinity. Choice D is the correct answer as it accurately compares the salinity of the two oceans based on the provided information. Choices B and C are less effective because they focus on general processes rather than making a direct comparison.

Answers are provided on page 218.

1

While researching a topic, a student has taken the following notes:

- The Health Data Repository (HDR) includes main biological markers and environmental factors for tracking diseases.
- Biological markers include traits such as gene expression and protein levels.
- Many prediction models use these biological markers to forecast disease outbreaks.
- These models may fail to accurately identify key markers in diseases with varying genetic profiles.
- Models based on environmental factors, such as climate and population density, are more reliable predictors of disease outbreaks.

The student wants to explain a disadvantage of relying on biological markers to predict disease outbreaks. Which choice most effectively uses relevant information from the notes to accomplish this goal?

A) Many prediction models are based on biological markers, such as gene expression and protein levels.

B) Models based on biological markers may misidentify key markers in diseases with varying genetic profiles, making such models less reliable predictors of outbreaks than those based on environmental factors.

C) Biological markers include traits such as gene expression and protein levels, which may vary within a disease, whereas environmental factors describe fixed traits like climate and population density, which are reliable predictors of outbreaks.

D) The HDR's environmental factors are reliable predictors of disease outbreaks, as the traits they describe are fixed.

2

While researching a topic, a student has taken the following notes:

- Tokyo is the capital of Japan.
- The city's population is around 9.73 million.
- Tokyo houses about 7.67% of Japan's total population.
- Seoul is the capital of South Korea.
- The city's population is around 9.86 million.
- Seoul contains approximately 19.09% of South Korea's total population.

Which choice most effectively uses information from the given sentences to emphasize the relative sizes of the populations in these two capitals?

A) Japan's capital, Tokyo, with a population of around 9.73 million, and South Korea's capital, Seoul, with a population of around 9.86 million, both house a significant portion of their respective country's populations.

B) Tokyo and Seoul are the capitals of Japan and South Korea, respectively, with respective populations of around 9.73 million and 9.86 million.

C) Despite Seoul having a larger population than Tokyo, Tokyo accounts for a smaller percentage of its country's total population.

D) Comparing Japan and South Korea, 9.73 million is 7.67% of Japan's total population, and 9.86 million is 19.09% of South Korea's.

8

PRACTICE TEST

- ❐ SET #1
- ❐ SET #2
- ❐ SET #3
- ❐ SET #4

Answers are provided on page 218~220.

1

1

Seeds in a greenhouse, a type of controlled environment for plant growth, are watered and exposed to light until they ________, at which point they are transferred to soil and given nutrients to continue growing into mature plants.

Which choice completes the text so that it conforms to the conventions of Standard English?

A) will germinate

B) germinate

C) had germinated

D) are germinating

2

Even though wolves are skilled hunters and can take down large prey, they usually ________ to hunt smaller animals like rabbits and rodents. A recent study explains why: smaller prey is easier to catch and require less energy to capture, making them a more efficient food source for wolves.

Which choice completes the text so that it conforms to the conventions of Standard English?

A) prefer

B) preferring

C) to prefer

D) have preferred

3

Acclaimed physicist Albert Einstein and engineer Mileva Maric significantly contributed to the development of the theory of relativity, a concept that ________ the fundamental principles of space, time, and gravity.

Which choice completes the text so that it conforms to the conventions of Standard English?

A) have depicted

B) were depicting

C) depicts

D) depict

4

The flowering period of different species of cherry blossoms can vary greatly. For example, some cherry blossom trees may bloom for just a few ________ others can remain in full bloom for several weeks.

Which choice completes the text so that it conforms to the conventions of Standard English?

A) days: while

B) days. While

C) days; while

D) days, while

5

The new anti-poaching ________ employs drones equipped with infrared cameras to track the movement of poachers in protected wildlife areas, allowing rangers to respond quickly and prevent poaching without risking human life.

Which choice completes the text so that it conforms to the conventions of Standard English?

A) technology, created, by wildlife conservationists in South Africa

B) technology created by wildlife conservationists in South Africa

C) technology created by wildlife conservationists in South Africa,

D) technology, created by wildlife conservationists in South Africa

6

Among the students who received scholarships from the foundation ________ John Smith, a young man from a small town in rural Iowa who had overcome significant obstacles to pursue his dream of becoming a doctor.

Which choice completes the text so that it conforms to the conventions of Standard English?

A) was

B) were

C) are

D) have been

7

Based on historical documents, scholars have generally agreed that the first printing press was invented in Europe in the fifteenth century. However, since discovering ancient Chinese texts describing movable type printing from the eleventh century, ________ may have been developed much earlier

Which choice completes the text so that it conforms to the conventions of Standard English?

A) researcher Qiu Zhonghui has argued that printing technology

B) researcher Qiu Zhonghui's argument is that printing technology

C) printing technology, researcher Qiu Zhonghui has argued,

D) the argument researcher Qiu Zhonghui has made is that printing technology

8

The Great Barrier Reef is a natural wonder off the coast of Australia and is the world's largest coral reef system. Marine biologist Emily Wong recently explored the Reef to study its diverse marine ________ over 2,300 kilometers, the reef is home to over 600 types of coral and thousands of species of fish.

Which choice completes the text so that it conforms to the conventions of Standard English?

A) life. Spanning

B) life, spanning

C) life and spanning

D) life spanning

9

Chemical engineer Ana Priscila García and her team at the National Autonomous University of Mexico have developed a method for capturing sulfur dioxide emissions using a slurry of the ________ reacts with sulfur dioxide to form solid calcium sulfite that can be easily removed from the flue gas.

Which choice completes the text so that it conforms to the conventions of Standard English?

A) chemical compound, calcium oxide which

B) chemical compound calcium oxide, which

C) chemical compound, calcium oxide, which

D) chemical compound—calcium oxide, which

10

We're trying to improve employee morale. ________ we're planning a company retreat to build teamwork and foster positive relationships among staff.

Which choice completes the text so that it conforms to the conventions of Standard English?

A) To that end,

B) Nevertheless,

C) Similarly,

D) Meanwhilc,

11

The new science center boasts state-of-the-art laboratories and a planetarium for astronomy enthusiasts. ________ it has a science library with a vast collection of research materials.

Which choice completes the text so that it conforms to the conventions of Standard English?

A) Indeed,

B) Still,

C) In addition,

D) For example,

12

The widespread use of disposable plastic products has led to a growing environmental crisis. ________ many governments and companies are taking steps to reduce plastic waste, such as banning single-use plastics and promoting recycling programs.

Which choice completes the text so that it conforms to the conventions of Standard English?

A) Therefore,

B) For example,

C) Indeed,

D) On the other hand,

13

While researching a topic, a student has taken the following notes:

- Two groundbreaking inventions significantly influenced the modern world.
- In 1879, Thomas Edison developed the practical electric light bulb, making electricity widely accessible for lighting.
- Edison's invention transformed everyday life by enabling productivity and safety after dark.
- In 1903, the Wright brothers achieved the first powered flight, marking the beginning of modern aviation.
- The Wright brothers' invention revolutionized transportation and global connectivity.

The student wants to emphasize a difference between the two inventions. Which choice most effectively uses relevant information from the notes to accomplish this goal?

A) Although both inventions revolutionized the modern world, Edison's light bulb focused on everyday life and safety, while the Wright brothers' airplane focused on transportation.

B) Edison's light bulb and the Wright brothers' airplane were both groundbreaking inventions that shaped the modern era.

C) In 1879, Edison developed the electric light bulb, and in 1903, the Wright brothers achieved powered flight.

D) Edison influenced the modern world by making the light bulb, and the Wright brothers by introducing powered flight.

14

While researching a topic, a student has taken the following notes:

- Sea turtles use ocean currents for transoceanic travel, which significantly reduces their energy expenditure.
- The mechanisms that aid this energy conservation while traveling were not completely known.
- Marine biologist Adriana Zavala used computer modeling to examine the effect of ocean currents on the travel of sea turtles.
- The study found that sea turtles are propelled in a specific direction by the current flow.
- Zavala deduced this propulsion decreases the impact of drag on the sea turtles by 124%.

The student wants to describe the study and its methodology. Which choice most effectively uses relevant information from the notes to achieve this?

A) A study uncovered that sea turtles, which spend up to 124% less energy when utilizing ocean currents for travel, also experience lesser drag.

B) In an attempt to comprehend how sea turtles save energy while using ocean currents for transoceanic travel, Adriana Zavala used computer modeling to examine the effect of these currents.

C) Adriana Zavala studied the mechanisms behind the fact that by being propelled in a specific direction by ocean currents, sea turtles conserve energy.

D) Marine biologist Adriana Zavala discovered that sea turtles are propelled in a specific direction by ocean currents, reducing the effect of drag by 124%.

15

While researching a topic, a student has taken the following notes:

- The Korean Wave, or "Hallyu," refers to the global popularity of South Korean culture, including music, television dramas, and movies.
- K-pop groups such as BTS and BLACKPINK have gained massive international followings, with BTS becoming the first Korean group to top the US Billboard 200 chart.
- South Korean television dramas, or "K-dramas," have attracted global audiences on streaming platforms like Netflix, with shows like Crash Landing on You and Squid Game gaining widespread popularity.
- Hallyu has significantly boosted South Korea's economy through the export of cultural products and increased tourism.
- The South Korean government actively supports Hallyu by promoting cultural exports and sponsoring Hallyu events worldwide.

The student wants to make and support a generalization about the Korean Wave. Which choice most effectively uses relevant information from the notes to accomplish this goal?

A) K-pop groups like BTS and BLACKPINK have gained massive international followings, illustrating the global appeal of South Korean music.

B) The global popularity of K-pop and K-dramas, supported by South Korean government efforts, has increased the country's cultural influence and boosted its economy through cultural exports and tourism.

C) South Korean television dramas, such as *Crash Landing on You* and *Squid Game*, have found large audiences on streaming services like Netflix.

D) The South Korean government's sponsorship of cultural exports and international events has helped promote the global popularity of Korean entertainment.

Answers are provided on page 220~221.

2

1

For centuries, people in the Pacific Islands ________ sweet potato, a starchy root vegetable, as a staple food source. Surprisingly, there is no historical evidence that any type of sweet potato is native to the Pacific Islands; it is believed that the plant was likely brought to the region by early Polynesian settlers.

Which choice completes the text so that it conforms to the conventions of Standard English?

A) have used

B) to use

C) using

D) uses

2

While many filmmakers aim to create movies with the latest technology and special ________ others opt for a more nostalgic approach, using practical effects and techniques from the early days of cinema.

Which choice completes the text so that it conforms to the conventions of Standard English?

A) effects. However,
B) effects but
C) effects,
D) effects, but

3

During the Great Depression, two struggling animators named William Hanna and Joseph Barbera decided to join forces to create cartoons together. After a few years of hard work and perseverance, they ________ their first cartoon series, Tom and Jerry, which went on to become one of the most successful and beloved animated shows of all time.

Which choice completes the text so that it conforms to the conventions of Standard English?

A) launch

B) launched

C) have launched

D) were launching

4

Marie Curie is perhaps best known for her pioneering work on radioactivity, which led to her winning two Nobel Prizes, but she also contributed greatly to the field of ________ mobile X-ray units for use on the front lines of World War I and training medical professionals in their use.

Which choice completes the text so that it conforms to the conventions of Standard English?

A) radiology, developing

B) radiology; developing

C) radiology. Developing

D) radiology developing

5

In analyzing the works of author Toni Morrison, ________ have overlooked her profound engagement with African American folklore and mythology.

Which choice completes the text so that it conforms to the conventions of Standard English?

A) many literary critics have focused on Morrison's treatment of race and gender but

B) Morrison's treatment of race and gender has been the focus of many critics, who

C) there is the focus on Morrison's treatment of race and gender literarily criticized by many and

D) there are many literary critics who have focused on Morrison's treatment of race and gender but

6

Recent studies of medieval manuscripts have led some researchers to propose that literacy rates in 12th-century Europe were higher than previously believed. This speculation ________ that widespread literacy extended beyond the clergy, nobility, and merchant class is untenable, historians Catherine Edwards and James Holloway counter, unless other explanations, such as the selective preservation of certain texts, can first be ruled out.

Which choice completes the text so that it conforms to the conventions of Standard English?

A) maintains

B) maintained

C) maintaining

D) has maintained

7

The centuries-old redwood trees of California's Muir Woods National Monument—majestic giants reaching towards ________ as a testament to nature's resilience. These towering trees have thrived in the region's foggy and moist climate, where the coastal mist envelops the forest floor, providing a nourishing environment for the redwoods to grow.

Which choice completes the text so that it conforms to the conventions of Standard English?

A) the sky stand

B) the sky: stand

C) the sky—stand

D) the sky, stand

8

The modern office space has undergone a significant transformation in recent years: gone are the drab cubicles and dull color schemes, replaced by open layouts, bold colors, and unique ________ game rooms and on-site cafes.

Which choice completes the text so that it conforms to the conventions of Standard English?

A) features such as:

B) features: such as

C) features, such as,

D) features such as

9

The menu at the new restaurant features a range of dishes from around the world: spaghetti alla carbonara, a classic Italian pasta ________ an Indonesian fried rice; and bibimbap, a Korean rice bowl topped with vegetables and meat.

Which choice completes the text so that it conforms to the conventions of Standard English?

A) dish, nasi goreng,

B) dish; nasi goreng,

C) dish; nasi goreng:

D) dish; nasi goreng

10

Scientists put forth the hypothesis that dolphins engage in cooperative play, a deliberate, repeated, and interactive ________ which these intelligent marine mammals strengthen social bonds, refine their communication skills, and enhance their cognitive abilities.

Which choice completes the text so that it conforms to the conventions of Standard English?

A) behavior, through

B) behavior. Through

C) behavior; through

D) behavior: through

11

Researchers have found that lack of sleep can have negative impacts on physical and mental health. ________ schools and employers are starting to prioritize healthy sleep habits, such as by adjusting schedules to allow for more rest.

Which choice completes the text so that it conforms to the conventions of Standard English?

A) Therefore,

B) Meanwhile,

C) Alternatively,

D) By the same token,

12

The athlcte completed the race with a personal best time. ________ she spoke to reporters about her training regimen and goals for the future.

Which choice completes the text so that it conforms to the conventions of Standard English?

A) By contrast,

B) Regardless,

C) As a result,

D) Afterward,

13

While researching a topic, a student has taken the following notes:

- Louisa May Alcott is a well-known American author.
- In 1868, she published Little Women, a novel about the lives of four sisters.
- The narrative portrays the learning and growth experiences in their normal domestic life.
- In 1871, she published Little Men, a novel following the lives of numerous boys in a school run by one of the Little Women characters.
- The stories depict the learning and growth experiences occurring in the school setting.

The student wants to underline a similarity between the two books by Louisa May Alcott. Which choice most effectively uses relevant information from the notes to accomplish this goal?

A) Louisa May Alcott's Little Women, portraying domestic adventures, contains fewer main characters than Little Men.

B) Little Women was published in 1868, and Little Men was published in 1871.

C) Unlike Little Men, Louisa May Alcott's Little Women is set in a domestic environment.

D) Louisa May Alcott's books Little Women and Little Men both portray growth and learning experiences in different environments.

14

While researching a topic, a student has taken the following notes:

- Research on influences affecting the hibernation cycle in mammals is well-established, but less is known about amphibians.
- A research group led by Dr. Heather Bleakley from Stanford University investigated the factors affecting amphibian hibernation.
- Dr. Bleakley's team collected hibernation and environmental data for over 2,000 amphibian species and utilized statistical models for analysis.
- Longer hibernation periods were linked with environments experiencing more drastic seasonal changes.
- Amphibians in these environments may hibernate longer to cope with extended periods of unfavorable conditions.

The student wants to emphasize the objective of the research study. Which choice most effectively uses relevant information from the notes to accomplish this goal?

A) The research team aimed to understand the factors influencing amphibian hibernation, as such factors have been well studied in mammals but not in amphibians.

B) After collecting data, researchers determined that longer hibernation periods were linked with environments experiencing more drastic seasonal changes.

C) The study concluded that amphibians in environments with greater seasonal change might hibernate longer to deal with extended periods of unfavorable conditions.

D) Researchers gathered hibernation and environmental data for over 2,000 amphibian species and analyzed the data using statistical models.

15

While researching a topic, a student has taken the following notes:

- Rising agents in baking cause carbon dioxide to be released within a dough, making the dough rise as it cooks.
- Yeast and sourdough starter are biological rising agents.
- Yeast is a single-celled microorganism.
- To produce carbon dioxide, yeast needs to be mixed with warm liquid and a sugar source such as honey.
- Sourdough starter is a mixture of wild yeast and bacteria.
- To produce carbon dioxide, a sourdough starter needs to be mixed with flour and water but not with a sugar source.

The student wants to emphasize a difference between yeast and a sourdough starter. Which choice most effectively uses relevant information from the notes to accomplish this goal?

A) In baking, rising agents like yeast and sourdough starter are used to make dough rise.

B) Yeast and sourdough starter are rising agents that, when mixed with other ingredients, cause carbon dioxide to be released within a dough.

C) Yeast is a single-celled microorganism, and honey is a type of sugar source.

D) To produce carbon dioxide within a dough, yeast needs to be mixed with a sugar source, whereas a sourdough starter does not.

Answers are provided on page 222~223.

3

1

________ suggest that over fifty percent of summer vacation packages are, in reality, tailor-made itineraries meticulously designed by travel experts, industry professionals who craft personalized trips according to individual preferences.

Which choice completes the text so that it conforms to the conventions of Standard English?

A) Travel agents' estimations'

B) Travel agents estimations'

C) Travel agents estimations

D) Travel agents' estimations

2

Like personal computers, smartphones have become an indispensable tool in today's digital age, enabling individuals to communicate, access information, and ________ a wide range of tasks conveniently from the palm of their hand.

Which choice completes the text so that it conforms to the conventions of Standard English?

A) performed

B) performing

C) would perform

D) perform

3

Despite encountering numerous challenges along its journey, Samsung Electronics persevered and emerged as a global leader in the technology industry. From its humble beginnings, Samsung has continuously pushed boundaries, introducing innovative products and solutions that ________ various sectors.

Which choice completes the text so that it conforms to the conventions of Standard English?

A) was revolutionizing

B) has revolutionized

C) have revolutionized

D) revolutionizes

4

Non-profit organization The Ocean Cleanup deals with ocean floating plastic wastes—tons of ________ their innovative cleanup operations.

Which choice completes the text so that it conforms to the conventions of Standard English?

A) them—through

B) them: through

C) them. Through

D) them through

5

In 1801, Samuel Taylor Coleridge, who was a key figure of the Romantic movement in English literature, ________ his famous poem "Kubla Khan."

Which choice completes the text so that it conforms to the conventions of Standard English?

A) had published

B) has published

C) would publish

D) published

6

While implementing new safety measures promotes workplace ________ argue that it can lead to a sense of restriction among employees and impose extra costs and administrative burdens on the organization.

Which choice completes the text so that it conforms to the conventions of Standard English?

A) security, but critics

B) security: critics

C) security; critics

D) security, critics

7

In 2018, while still a student, Emma embarked on an ambitious entrepreneurial venture, founding her own tech startup. Despite juggling coursework and exams, ________ to developing her business concept, securing funding, and assembling a talented team.

Which choice completes the text so that it conforms to the conventions of Standard English?

A) Emma's countless hours were dedicated

B) countless hours of Emma's dedication

C) Emma dedicated countless hours

D) countless hours Emma dedicated were

8

Despite the advancements in technology, machines themselves do not possess the ability to think or make ________ it is becoming increasingly apparent that many researchers and experts in the field of artificial intelligence envision a future where machines can exhibit advanced cognitive capabilities, leading to the development of intelligent systems capable of complex reasoning and decision-making processes.

Which choice completes the text so that it conforms to the conventions of Standard English?

A) decisions, however;

B) decisions. However,

C) decisions, however,

D) decisions however

9

The team has identified several critical impurities in the chemical formulation that need immediate attention. _______ we have decided to postpone the product release by two weeks to ensure a quality outcome.

Which choice completes the text with the most logical transition?

A) With this in mind,

B) In other words,

C) In fact,

D) All in all,

10

Many members of the US Supreme Court have voiced concerns about broadcasting their proceedings, fearing that it could affect the seriousness and authenticity of courtroom discussions. They worry that the presence of cameras might encourage theatrical behavior rather than sober legal debate. _____, some argue that broadcasting proceedings could enhance public understanding of the judicial process and promote transparency.

Which choice completes the text with the most logical transition?

A) In addition,

B) As such,

C) Similarly,

D) That said,

11

Harriet Tubman, a renowned African American abolitionist and political activist, wanted to eradicate the institution of slavery and ensure that all individuals, regardless of their race or background, could live in a world free from oppression and injustice. ________ she actively participated in the Underground Railroad, risking her own safety to guide enslaved individuals to freedom.

Which choice completes the text with the most logical transition?

A) Finally,

B) To that end,

C) In short,

D) In comparison,

12

Some technological innovations have crossed the line into everyday life as advancements in research and development have proven their usefulness and reliability. ________ smartphones are now commonly used for a range of purposes beyond communication, such as accessing information, managing schedules, and even monitoring health.

Which choice completes the text with the most logical transition?

A) For instance,

B) Even so,

C) Besides,

D) By contrast,

13

While researching a topic, a student has taken the following notes:

- Trees in urban areas can reduce temperatures by as much as 5°C through a process called transpiration.
- The physics behind transpiration's cooling effect hasn't always been well understood.
- Environmental scientist Dr. Maya Patel used climate models to study how urban tree transpiration affects local air temperatures.
- Patel's study revealed that trees release water vapor, which cools the surrounding air by absorbing heat as it evaporates.
- The study also found that areas with dense tree coverage experience up to 25% more cooling than areas with sparse vegetation.

The student wants to present the study and its methodology. Which choice most effectively uses relevant information from the notes to accomplish this goal?

A) A study revealed that trees in urban areas can reduce temperatures by as much as 5°C, with areas of dense tree coverage experiencing up to 25% more cooling.

B) Seeking to understand how urban trees reduce local air temperatures, Dr. Maya Patel used climate models to study the effects of tree transpiration on surrounding air.

C) Dr. Maya Patel studied the cooling effect of trees in urban areas, focusing on how transpiration releases water vapor and reduces air temperature.

D) Environmental scientist Dr. Maya Patel discovered that trees cool the air by releasing water vapor through transpiration, which reduces local temperatures by up to 5°C.

14

While researching a topic, a student has taken the following notes:

- Egypt's Great Pyramid of Giza was constructed around 2560 BC as a tomb for the Pharaoh Khufu.
- It has been a prominent archaeological site for centuries.
- Lidar (Light Detection and Ranging) is a cutting-edge remote sensing method that uses light in the form of a pulsed laser to measure distances.
- Archaeologist Dr. Maria Nilsson applied Lidar technology to photographs she had taken of the Great Pyramid's interior chambers.
- Nilsson's analysis unveiled numerous hidden passages and rooms unknown to researchers.

The student wants to introduce Nilsson's research to an audience unfamiliar with the Great Pyramid of Giza. Which choice most effectively uses relevant information from the notes to accomplish this goal?

A) Dr. Nilsson photographed the interior chambers of the Great Pyramid and then applied Lidar technology to the photographs.

B) Lidar is a cutting-edge remote sensing method that Dr. Nilsson used to enhance the detail in photographs of the Great Pyramid.

C) Using Lidar technology, Dr. Nilsson revealed numerous hidden passages and rooms within the Great Pyramid of Giza, one of Egypt's most significant archaeological sites.

D) Constructed as a tomb for Pharaoh Khufu, Egypt's Great Pyramid of Giza concealed numerous hidden passages and rooms unveiled by Lidar technology.

15

While researching a topic, a student has taken the following notes:

- The *cheongsam* is a body-hugging one-piece Chinese dress for women.
- It originated in Shanghai in the 1920s.
- The name "*cheongsam*" comes from the Cantonese word, meaning "long shirt".
- It is popularized by socialites and upper-class women.
- Combines elements of traditional Chinese garments and Western fashion.

The student wants to explain the origin of the word "*cheongsam*." Which choice most effectively uses relevant information from the notes to accomplish this goal?

A) The *cheongsam*, a stylish dress popularized in 1920s Shanghai, combines traditional Chinese and Western fashion elements.

B) The *cheongsam*, meaning "long shirt" in Cantonese, is a body-hugging dress that originated in Shanghai.

C) Socialites and upper-class women in Shanghai popularized the *cheongsam*, a one-piece Chinese dress.

D) Originating in the 1920s, the *cheongsam* became a fashionable dress among women in Shanghai.

4

Answers are provided on page 223~224.

1

As the climate changes, the impact on ecosystems can be assessed by comparing the ________ of current populations to that of historical records. When researchers analyzed the DNA of ancient plant specimens, they discovered similar genetic mutations occurring in both the past and present populations, indicating parallel adaptation to environmental shifts.

Which choice completes the text so that it conforms to the conventions of Standard English?

A) species' diversity's

B) species diversity's

C) specie's diversity

D) species' diversity

2

Advised strategies for eliminating glue from a wooden surface include scrubbing, cooling the glue with ice to facilitate ________ removal, and applying a variety of solvents to loosen its adherence. Additionally, employing heat via a hairdryer can also help to soften the glue, making it easier to wipe off.

Which choice completes the text so that it conforms to the conventions of Standard English?

A) their

B) its

C) its'

D) there

3

Sejong the Great, also known as King Sejong, is celebrated for his creation of the Korean alphabet, known as Hangul, with the aim of enhancing literacy among the common people. Hangul, revered among linguists, ________ for its remarkable and inventive design

Which choice completes the text so that it conforms to the conventions of Standard English?

A) having stood out

B) to stand out

C) stands out

D) standing out

4

When organizing large-scale festivals, event coordinators secure suitable venues, manage ticket sales, and ________ food availability, beverage offerings, and serving arrangements.

Which choice completes the text so that it conforms to the conventions of Standard English?

A) ensure

B) ensuring

C) and ensure

D) while ensuring

5

By studying aerospace, scientists and engineers delve into the intricacies of flight, propulsion, and space ________ the foundation for advancements in aircraft and spacecraft design, technology, and exploration of the cosmos.

Which choice completes the text with the most logical transition?

A) exploration, laying

B) exploration laying

C) exploration; laying

D) exploration. Laying

6

By conducting thorough research and analysis of historical data, ________ informed predictions, reducing the need for risky investments and increasing the chances of financial success.

Which choice completes the text with the most logical transition?

A) economists can gain valuable insights into market trends and make

B) economists' valuable insights into market trends can be gained, and they make

C) valuable insights into market trends can be gained by economists, making

D) gaining valuable insights into market trends can be done by economists, and they make

7

Contrary to the conventional view of AI, ________ it as a threat to human employment, Dr. Kim emphasizes its potential as a collaborative tool that can empower individuals and drive innovation in various fields.

Which choice completes the text with the most logical transition?

A) portraying

B) this portrays

C) which portrays

D) it portrays

8

How individuals navigate through challenging situations and overcome adversity, drawing upon their resilience and inner ________ not always fully appreciated or recognized by those around them.

Which choice completes the text with the most logical transition?

A) strength: is

B) strength is

C) strength; is

D) strength, is

9

Applicants to many prestigious high schools must pass two ________ focusing on academic proficiency and another assessing critical thinking skills and problem-solving abilities.

Which choice completes the text with the most logical transition?

A) exams while one

B) exams; one

C) exams. One

D) exams: one

10

Mental health is gaining more attention and awareness in society. ________ employers are implementing programs to support the mental health of their employees and reduce stigma surrounding mental illness.

Which choice completes the text with the most logical transition?

A) To that end,

B) Also,

C) Increasingly,

D) Particularly,

11

Due to the effects of climate change, many coastal communities are experiencing more frequent and severe flooding. ________ architects and city planners are designing buildings and infrastructure that can withstand rising sea levels and storms.

Which choice completes the text with the most logical transition?

A) Similarly,

B) Therefore,

C) Conversely,

D) Even so,

12

The shapes and items that can be carved out of ivory from teeth and tusks are practically endless. Small statues, netsukes, jewelry, flatware handles, furniture inlays, and piano keys are a few miniature examples of carved ivory items. ________ it is possible to scrimshaw or superficially carve wart hog tusks, sperm whale, killer whale, and hippopotamus teeth while maintaining their original shapes as morphologically recognized items.

Which choice completes the text with the most logical transition?

A) Additionally,

B) Finally,

C) Increasingly,

D) However,

13

While researching a topic, a student has taken the following notes:

- The Travels of Marco Polo was a popular book in medieval Europe, detailing Marco Polo's adventures in Asia.
- The book described a mythical land called Cathay, believed to be rich in gold and jewels.
- European explorers, including Christopher Columbus, sought a direct route to Asia to reach Cathay and other wealthy realms.
- Believing Asia to be closer to Europe than it actually is, Columbus set sail westward and eventually landed in what is now known as the Americas.
- The term "Cathay" was commonly used until the 17th century when more accurate maps of Asia were developed.

The student wants to emphasize the role a misconception played in the exploration of new territories. Which choice most effectively uses relevant information from the notes to accomplish this goal?

A) The Travels of Marco Polo introduced Europeans to Cathay, a mythical land of riches that drove the age of exploration.

B) Christopher Columbus sought to reach Cathay, a land of wealth described by Marco Polo, which led him to discover the Americas.

C) The book The Travels of Marco Polo misled explorers like Columbus into believing that Asia was much closer to Europe.

D) Motivated by descriptions of Cathay in The Travels of Marco Polo, Columbus embarked on his voyage, leading to the accidental discovery of the Americas.

14

While researching a topic, a student has taken the following notes:

- The Arctic fox (Vulpes lagopus) is remarkably adapted to survive in extremely cold climates.
- Its diet is diverse, including small mammals like lemmings, as well as birds, fish, and carrion.
- One survival strategy of the Arctic fox is to follow polar bears and scavenge the remains of their kills.
- The fox also adapts during periods of food scarcity by foraging in human settlements, often rummaging through garbage.
- This scavenging behavior increases during the winter months when traditional food sources are more scarce.

The student wants to emphasize a similarity between the two survival strategies of the Arctic fox. Which choice most effectively uses relevant information from the notes to accomplish this goal?

A) The Arctic fox, adept in cold climates, mainly consumes small mammals, but its diet varies to include birds and fish.

B) Both of the Arctic fox's survival strategies involve scavenging for food: following polar bears for leftovers and rummaging through human garbage, especially in winter.

C) While the Arctic fox predominantly hunts small mammals, it also follows polar bears and searches human settlements for food during times of scarcity.

D) In response to the harsh climate, the Arctic fox scavenges after polar bears and in human areas, particularly during the winter when food is less available.

15

While researching a topic, a student has taken the following notes:

- The Ainu are an indigenous group who have lived in parts of northern Japan and Russia since ancient times.
- Ainu culture has influences from Jomon and Okhotsk civilizations.
- Hiroshi Maruyama is an Ainu historian, educator, and advocate.
- He founded the Ainu Museum of Nibutani, Hokkaido, Japan, in 1990.
- Masaaki Sugita is an Ainu historian, artist, and advocate.
- He founded the Ainu Museum of Chitose, Hokkaido, Japan, in 1992.

The student wants to emphasize the length and purpose of Maruyama's and Sugita's work. Which choice most effectively uses relevant information from the notes to accomplish this goal?

A) At the Ainu Museums in Nibutani and Chitose, Hokkaido, visitors can learn more about the Ainu people who have lived in the region since ancient times.

B) Hiroshi Maruyama and Masaaki Sugita have dedicated their lives to preserving the culture of the Ainu people, who have lived in parts of northern Japan and Russia for centuries.

C) Since the early 1990s, Hiroshi Maruyama and Masaaki Sugita have worked to protect Ainu culture through their museums.

D) Influenced by the traditions of Jomon and Okhotsk civilizations, Ainu culture has existed in parts of northern Japan and Russia since ancient times.

9

ANSWERS

- ❏ DRILLS
- ❏ PROBLEM SET

Answers to the Noun Drill

1> Nature's splendor [S] has captivated me for my entire life [S]. It's breathtaking to see the mighty mountains [P] with their soaring summits [P]. The vibrant flowers [P] that adorn the meadows [P] make me happy. I can't help but be in awe [S] of the calm [S] of the flowing water [S] as I stroll along the riverbank [S]. The chirping [S] of birds [P] in the sky [S] contributes to nature's melody [S]. The limbs [P] of each tree [S] in the forest [S] reach upward to tell a different tale [S]. I am constantly in awe [S] of nature's marvels [P], from the tiniest pebble [S] to the largest waterfall [S].

2> I like experimenting [S] with different recipes [P] in my kitchen [S]. I made the decision [S] to make chocolate-chip cookies [P] today. I took great care [S] when measuring the flour [S], sugar [S], and butter [S]. The perfume [S] of vanilla extract [S] permeated the room [S] as I stirred the dough [S]. As I melted the chocolate chips [P] into the mixture [S], I added them. I then rolled the dough [S] into small balls [P] and put them on a baking sheet [S]. The cookies [P] started to become golden brown after a few minutes [S] in the oven [S]. I couldn't wait to share the batch's twelve delectable delights [P] with my family [S] and friends [P]. Baking [S] is more than simply a pastime [S]; it's a great way [S] to make appetizing treats [P] and cheer up other people [P].

3> Sarah is a voracious antique book collector [S]. Each book [S] on her shelves [P] tells a different story [S] and is rich with gems [P]. She admires the elaborate pictures [P] and meticulously maintained texts [P] as she turns the pages [P]. Sarah takes pride [S] in the range [S] of genres [P] that are represented in her collection [S], which includes historical biographies [P] and classic novels [P]. Each new item [S] she adds to her collection [S] makes her happy and excited. Whenever people [P] come over, they are in awe [S] of the enormous variety [S] of literary treasures [P] that line her bookcases [P]. Sarah's love [S] of reading [S] and the pleasure [S] it offers her is evident in her passion [S] for book collecting [S].

Answers to the Pronoun Drill 1

1> Sulfur dioxide causes acid rain, which damages crops and forests, and contributes to respiratory problems in humans and animals, particularly in those with asthma or other lung diseases.

2> Juliet met Romeo, who is the old foe of her family, and she fell deeply in love with him, despite the longstanding ~~feud between~~ their families.

3> Art critics who write for mainstream publications often need to balance their own personal opinions about an artwork with the broader public's perception and understanding of it.

4> Some carried briefcases, others had backpacks slung over their shoulder.

5> Superman, whose story dates back to the late 1930s, is known for his extraordinary powers and commitment to justice.

Answers to the Pronoun Drill 2

1> The masterpiece painting "Mona Lisa" by Leonardo da Vinci is celebrated for its artistic brilliance, but we must remember that (**his**/our) creation was made possible through the use of various techniques and skills employed by da Vinci and other artists of the Renaissance era.

2> Susan has captivated readers with her compelling storytelling and vivid imagination. She finds inspiration for (**her**/their) creative works in a variety of experiences and sources.

Answers to the Pronoun Drill 2 (cont.)

3> Ecologists have studied how certain plants can close (itself/**themselves**) up in response to touch or disturbances, protecting their delicate flowers or leaves from potential harm.

4> Linda has been a driving force behind several successful social initiatives. Her dedication and passion for making a positive change in the world have motivated others to join (**her**/their) cause.

5> The renowned artists Pablo Picasso and Georges Braque are often credited with the invention of Cubism, but (their/**its**) development was influenced by the artistic experiments of predecessors such as Paul Cézanne and Henri Matisse.

6> Researchers have discovered that certain types of orchids have the ability to change (them/**themselves**) in response to environmental conditions, allowing them to adapt to different pollinators.

7> As a candidate for the position, what qualities and skills make (**me**/myself) a strong fit for this role?

8> Researcher Maria Garcia argues that public health campaigns promoting regular exercise can yield positive outcomes, particularly when thesc campaigns provide individuals with options: for example, a study showed that gym attendance increased by 30% after individuals were asked whether (**they**/he) wanted to join fitness classes.

9> When it comes to personal growth and development, certain strategies and practices have helped (**me**/myself) overcome challenges and achieve success.

10> Scientists have found that certain species of lizards can detach (them/**themselves**) from their tails as a defense mechanism, distracting predators while the lizards make a quick escape.

11> Environmental organizations stress that awareness campaigns on sustainable transportation can have a significant impact, particularly when these campaigns emphasize the importance of eco-friendly options: for example, a town experienced a rise in bicycle ridership after residents were asked whether (**they**/it) would consider cycling for short distances.

Answers to the Adjective & Adverb Drill

ADJ
1> She sang a beautiful song.

ADV ADV
2> He ran quickly to catch the bus.

ADV ADJ
3> The cake tasted deliciously sweet.

ADJ ADV ADV
4> The lazy cat slept peacefully on the windowsill.

ADV ADV
5> The sun shone brightly on the sandy beach.

Answers to the Preposition Drill

1> If radioactive water (from a damaged power plant) is released, it can have serious consequences (for human health and the environment), (depending on the amount and type) (of radioactive material released and the location) (of the release).

2> The potential health risks (of exposure to radioactive water) include radiation sickness, cancer, genetic mutations, and other health problems.

3> Additionally, the release (of radioactive water) can also have long-term environmental impacts, (such as contamination) (of soil, water, and food sources), (as well as harm) (to wildlife and marine ecosystems).

4> It's important to note that the consequences (of a release) (of radioactive water) can be severe and long-lasting.

5> Therefore, it's crucial to take all necessary measures to prevent such incidents and to properly manage radioactive waste to minimize the risk (of such accidents) (in the future).

Answers to the Verb Drill

HV HV AV HV AV
1> I should have practiced more to improve my skills and be better prepared for the challenge ahead.

HV HV AV
2> The population of Amur tigers has been severely depleted due to habitat loss, poaching, and human encroachment.

3> The XYZ company $\underset{\text{HV}}{\text{is}}$ still $\underset{\text{AV}}{\text{deciding}}$ on the best course of action to take in response to the changing market conditions and evolving customer needs.

4> Malcolm X $\underset{\text{LV}}{\text{was}}$ a prominent civil rights leader and activist in the United States during the mid-20th century.

5> Thomas Paines speech $\underset{\text{LV}}{\text{sounded}}$ eloquent, impactful, and resonant with powerful rhetoric.

6> The apple that the witch $\underset{\text{AV}}{\text{gave}}$ to Snow White $\underset{\text{LV}}{\text{tasted}}$ sweet, but it $\underset{\text{HV}}{\text{was}}$ $\underset{\text{AV}}{\text{laced}}$ with a deadly poison.

Answers to the Conjunction Drill

1> The politician emphasized in her speech $\underset{\text{NC}}{\text{that}}$ her policies would $\underset{\text{CO}}{\text{not only}}$ (benefit the economy) $\underset{\text{CO}}{\text{but also}}$ ((prioritize social justice) $\underset{\text{CC}}{\text{and}}$ (environmental protection)).

2> The university's mission statement highlights its commitment $\underset{\text{CO}}{\text{not only}}$ (to academic excellence) $\underset{\text{CO}}{\text{but also}}$ (to (diversity) $\underset{\text{CC}}{\text{and}}$ (inclusion among its student (body) $\underset{\text{CC}}{\text{and}}$ (faculty))).

3> The hotel's website promotes its dedication $\underset{\text{CO}}{\text{not only}}$ (to luxurious (amenities) $\underset{\text{CC}}{\text{and}}$ (comfort)) $\underset{\text{CO}}{\text{but also}}$ (to (sustainability) $\underset{\text{CC}}{\text{and}}$ (eco-friendliness)).

4> Sarah, $\underset{\text{ADJC}}{\text{who}}$ cried all night long, finally (fell asleep in the early hours of the morning) $\underset{\text{CC}}{\text{and}}$ (woke up feeling (exhausted) $\underset{\text{CC}}{\text{and}}$ (emotionally drained)).

5> The book, $\underset{\text{ADJC}}{\text{which}}$ was written by a famous author, has received rave reviews from critics around the world $\underset{\text{ADVC}}{\text{because}}$ it (tackles important social issues) $\underset{\text{CC}}{\text{and}}$ (offers a fresh perspective on the human condition).

6> $\underset{\text{ADVC}}{\text{While}}$ Jake was in the bathroom, (his phone rang incessantly), $\underset{\text{CC}}{\text{and}}$ (he missed several important calls from his boss).

7> Sarah (received a gift $\underset{\text{ADJC}}{\text{that}}$ her boyfriend prepared for Valentine's Day) $\underset{\text{CC}}{\text{and}}$ (loved it).

8> Sarah received a gift $\underset{\text{ADJC}}{\text{that}}$ her boyfriend (prepared for Valentine's Day) $\underset{\text{CC}}{\text{and}}$ (was excited to give as a token of his (love) $\underset{\text{CC}}{\text{and}}$ (appreciation)).

9> $\underset{\text{NC}}{\text{That}}$ Vicky got a perfect score on the SAT made her parents extremely proud of her.

Answers to the Verb Tense Problem Set

1> A) was
2> D) had finished
3> B) will remain
4> B) remain
5> B) were
6> B) are
7> C) would fill
8> C) caused
9> B) have scored
10> D) would whistle
11> C) would never smoke
12> B) has been
13> B) flourished
14> C) had passed

Answers to the Verb Voice Drill 1

1> The floor is being swept by the janitor.

2> Not possible

3> A beautiful rendition of the classic ballad was sung by Mariah.

4> The plans for the new building were meticulously drafted by Architect Mike.

5> The flaws in the dish were quickly identified by Gordon Ramsay's expert palate.

Answers to the Verb Voice Drill 2

1> All students will be given opportunities to express their thoughts on this matter. **Passive voice**

2> The company has implemented several new policies and procedures to improve efficiency and ensure compliance with industry regulations. **Active voice**

3> For your convenience, a user-friendly interface has been designed with intuitive navigation and clear labeling to ensure ease of use for all users. **Passive voice**

4> All requirements must be met in order for prospective students to be considered for admission into the program. **Passive Voice**

5> Microhard has installed a new security system to protect their confidential data. **Active Voice**

6> By joining the company's loyalty program, customers can earn points for their purchases and redeem them for exclusive rewards and discounts. **Active Voice**

Answers to the Verbid Drill 1

PAR V. PAR PAR
1> The tree planted in the backyard grew tall and strong, providing shade and beauty to the surrounding area.

PAR V.
2> The new security system installed at the office building includes state-of-the-art surveillance cameras, motion sensors, and access control measures.

PAR V.
3> Easy-to-follow assembly instructions included in the product box made it simple and straightforward for the customer to assemble the product at home without the need for any additional tools or equipment.

PAR V. PAR
4> The actress cast in Resident Evil impressed audiences and critics alike with her compelling portrayal of the iconic protagonist.

V. V.
5> Gold fascinated people in California during the mid-19th century because it was believed to be a source of immense wealth and opportunity.

Answers to the Verbid Drill 2

PAR
1> With the increasing use of technology among children, many parents are turning to software that allows
INF
them to monitor their kids' online activities and set restrictions on screen time.

PAR GER
2> John Muir, a renowned conservationist, dedicated his life to protecting and preserving natural landscapes.

PAR
3> While having dinner at a fancy restaurant, the couple enjoyed a delicious meal of prime rib and lobster,
PAR
accompanied by a bottle of fine wine and a decadent dessert.

PAR
4> Many juries objected to the prosecution's evidence, citing a lack of credibility and insufficient proof
INF
to support the charges.

PAR INF
5> Having diverse facial expressions, Kimberly was able to effectively convey her emotions and thoughts during her presentation.

PAR PAR
6> Understanding Albert Einstein's theory of relativity is crucial for grasping the fundamental nature of
GER
space, time, and gravity, and for unlocking new insights into the workings of the universe.

Answers to the Verbid Problem Set

1> **The correct answer is B**

The infinitive form "to address" is used to express the purpose or goal of the engineers and scientists' ongoing work.

2> **The correct answer is D**

In this context, "aimed to discover" expresses the team's intention or goal to achieve a breakthrough treatment. The infinitive form "to discover" is used to indicate the purpose of their efforts.

3> **The correct answer is A**

The gerund form "repenting" is used for the object of the preposition "of."

4> **The correct answer is A**

In this context, "to garner" is the appropriate phrase to express the volunteers' objective or intention to obtain or gather widespread support. The infinitive form "to garner" is used to indicate the purpose or goal of their efforts.

5> **The correct answer is B**

The infinitive form "to uncover" is used to express the purpose or goal of the research team's study. It indicates that the team conducted the study with the aim of discovering or revealing the root causes and potential solutions for the high unemployment rates in the local community.

6> **The correct answer is C**

A period is needed to break two independent clauses.

7> **The correct answer is B**

The phrase "to create" is used to express the purpose or goal of the landscape architects and urban planners' design efforts. The infinitive form "to create" indicates their intention or objective of crafting a serene and harmonious environment within the park.

8> **The correct answer is A**

The infinitive form "to accomplish" is an idiomatic way to express the purpose or goal after the verb "allow".

9> **The correct answer is C**

A period is needed to break two independent clauses.

10> **The correct answer is D**

In this context, the present participle form "delivering" is used to describe the ongoing action of volunteers and organizations actively engaged in delivering relief supplies and providing assistance.

11> **The correct answer is A**

The gerund form "creating" is used for the object of the preposition "to."

12> **The correct answer is D**

The gerund form "building" is used for the object of the preposition "in."

Answers to the Participle & Appositive Drill

1> The Deep Sea Research Institute has secured one of the largest government funding, [P] allowing it to begin the preliminary research.

2> ACV corporation implemented a new policy, [A] a four-day workweek, [P] hoping to boost employee morale.

3> Samsung has recently released a new product line, [A] a high-performance laptop, [P] expanding its market reach.

4> Yuna Kim broke the world record, [A] a feat that had never been accomplished before, [P] inspiring a new generation of competitors.

5> Galileo Galilei is perhaps best known for inventing an early microscope and observing planets and stars, but he also dedicated himself to physics, [A] the study of motion and force, [P] demonstrating that the speed of fall of a heavy object is not proportional to its weight.

Answers to the Relative Conjunction Drill

1> who
2> at which
3> in which
4> at which
5> by which
6> in which
7> from which
8> on which
9> on which
10> to which

Answers to the Relative Conjunction Problem Set

1> The correct answer is D
The use of 'whose' in this context is referring to the 'civilizations' mentioned earlier in the sentence. It effectively conveys that the artifacts and cultural remnants from these civilizations were used to reconstruct their history.

2> The correct answer is A
This choice flows smoothly and maintains subject-verb agreement. It also correctly uses "whose" to refer back to "novels," indicating that the chapters of these novels ended with cliffhangers. Other options either create sentence fragments or awkward constructions (e.g., "each of these chapters had a cliffhanger endings" has a pluralization error).

Answers to the Comma Drill

1> In her analysis of Jane Austen's novel *Pride and Prejudice*, literary scholar Emma Thompson highlights how the book depicts the social conventions and constraints of Regency-era England, a period defined by strict social hierarchies, limited choices for women, and societal expectations based on class and wealth.

2> The invention of the Post-it Note can be traced back to a 3M scientist named Spencer Silver, who created a low-tack, reusable adhesive in the late 1960s. However, it wasn't until several years later that a colleague named Art Fry realized the adhesive's potential as a bookmark.

3> The idea for the Dyson vacuum cleaner came to inventor James Dyson in the 1970s, when he became frustrated with the poor performance of his own vacuum. After years of experimentation and refinement, Dyson developed a unique cyclonic system that revolutionized the way we think about vacuuming.

4> The invention of the modern automobile can be attributed to several different inventors and innovators, including Karl Benz, Gottlieb Daimler, and Henry Ford. However, it wasn't until Ford's introduction of the assembly line in the early 1900s that cars became affordable and accessible to the average person.

5> Throughout history, people in many cultures have used herbal remedies to treat common ailments such as headaches, indigestion, and colds. While modern medicine has largely replaced the use of herbs in clinical settings, herbal remedies continue to be a popular choice for people seeking natural alternatives to pharmaceutical drugs.

Answers to the Semicolon Drill

1> The serene stillness of the evening enveloped the landscape, creating a peaceful **atmosphere; residents** strolled along the quiet streets, enjoying the tranquility of the moment.

2 > The potential contamination of rainwater with uranium, resulting from the release of supposedly-treated radioactive water, raises notable environmental and health **concerns; proper** scrutiny, monitoring, and effective treatment methods are crucial to mitigate the risks associated with this issue and protect both the ecosystem and human health.

3> The release of toxic pollutants into the air from industrial emissions poses substantial environmental and public health **risks; implementing** strict emission standards is an essential measure to mitigate these concerns and protect both the environment and the well-being of nearby communities.

4> Inspired by her personal experiences, renowned author Maya Angelou dedicated herself to advocating for civil rights and social justice throughout her **life; her** tireless work included delivering powerful speeches, penning influential books, and using her creative talents to shed light on the struggles faced by marginalized communities.

5> Considering the higher occurrence of a particular enzyme variant in individuals with a heightened sense of taste, some researchers suggest that its function is not **passive; rather**, it may actively contribute to the perception and discrimination of flavors.

Answers to the Punctuation Problem Set

1> C
2> A
3> D
4> B
5> D
6> B
7> A
8> A
9> C
10> D
11> A
12> D

Answers to the Subject & Verb Drill

1> Devastated by war and displacement, the resilient communities, with their vibrant cultures and deep-rooted traditions, (is/**are**) now striving for recovery and rebuilding.

2> The number of students enrolled in the university (**has**/have) steadily increased over the past decade, with over 30,000 students currently attending.

3> Against the wall (hangs/**hang**) several paintings that caught everyone's attention.

4> Both Daniel, who is an accomplished pianist, and Sarah, who is a skilled violinist, (has/**have**) met the conductor to discuss their upcoming collaboration in order to meet the high artistic expectations of the upcoming performance.

5> The long-term benefits of a healthy diet on physical and mental health (is/**are**) well documented by scientific studies.

6> The harmful effects of prolonged sitting on posture and musculoskeletal health (is/**are**) increasingly well documented by medical research.

7> Beside the fireplace (sits/**sit**) the family dogs, warming themselves on a cold winter evening.

8> Severely impacted by overfishing and climate change, the once teeming fish populations, with their shimmering scales and graceful movements, (is/**are**) now experiencing a steady decline.

9> The positive effects of mindfulness meditation on stress reduction and emotional regulation (is/**are**) becoming increasingly well documented by scientific studies.

10> The Palace of Versailles, a sumptuous royal residence built in the 17th century, (**is**/are) located just outside of Paris and is one of the most popular tourist attractions in France.

11> Beneath the surface of the water (swims/**swim**) graceful dolphins.

12> The Acropolis, a citadel and ancient monument located in Athens, Greece, (**overlooks**/overlook) the city and offers stunning views of the surrounding landscape.

13> Surprisingly little (**is**/are) known about the long-term effects of social media on mental health despite its widespread use among people of all ages.

14> On the edge of the cliff (stands/**stand**) tourists taking photos.

15> Ravaged by wildfires and deforestation, the lush rainforests, adorned with a rich diversity of plant and animal species, (is/**are**) now facing the risk of irreversible destruction.

16> Devastated by war and displacement, the resilient communities, with their vibrant cultures and deep-rooted traditions, (is/**are**) now striving for recovery and rebuilding.

17> Near the entrance to the park (sits/**sit**) homeless men begging for spare change.

18> Deeply affected by pollution and habitat loss, the delicate coral reefs, adorned with vibrant colors and intricate formations, (is/**are**) now displaying early signs of regeneration.

19> Sarah's paintings of the coastal landscapes (reflects/**reflect**) a profound fascination with and appreciation for the ever-changing colors and textures of the sea.

20> From the top of the mountains (**comes**/come) a loud, piercing scream every day.

21> The number of people living in poverty (**has**/have) decreased significantly in many parts of the world due to various government programs and economic growth.

Answers to the Run-On & Fragment Drill

1> run-on
2> fragment
3> fragment
4> fragment
5> run-on
6> run-on
7> conjunction redundancy
8> run-on
9> run-on
10> fragment
11> fragment
12> conjunction redundancy
13> run-on
14> fragment
15> run-on
16> run-on
17> run-on
18> conjunction redundancy

Answers to the Comparison Problem Set

1> **The correct answer is C.**
Option C, "than do traditional gasoline-powered cars," completes the sentence correctly in the context of the comparison being made. This choice makes clear that the comparison is between electric vehicles (EVs) and traditional gasoline-powered cars in terms of their respective contributions to air pollution and greenhouse gas emissions. The use of "do" in this context serves to implicitly carry forward the verb phrase "offer a greener and more sustainable mode of transportation" from the first part of the sentence, making the sentence both clear and grammatically correct.

The other options either introduce ambiguity (A and B could be interpreted to mean the act of selecting the cars contributes to pollution) or create an inappropriate comparison (D compares people who choose electric vehicles to people who choose traditional cars, rather than comparing the vehicles themselves).

2> **The correct answer is A.**
It completes the comparison between the educational journey of dental hygienists and dentists. The phrase "that of dentists" indicates that we are comparing the educational journey of dental hygienists to that of dentists. The sentence states that the educational journey for dental hygienists is considerably shorter than the educational journey of dentists.

3> **The correct answer is C.**
It directly compares an area with the Amazon rainforest.

4> **The correct answer is C.**
The sentence is comparing individuals who reported consuming berries at least five times per week with a group of individuals who reported not consuming any berries. The phrase "those who reported no berry..." accurately represents the group that did not consume any berries.

5> **The correct answer is D.**
The sentence compares the students who engaged in hands-on robotics projects with the students who did not participate in such activities.

6> **The correct answer is B.**
The sentence compares the artists of preceding eras with the artists like Leonardo da Vinci and Michelangelo.

7> **The correct answer is B.**
The sentence compares the performance of Chris with the performance of other candidates.

8> **The correct answer is C.**
The sentence compares nocturnal animals with diurnal animals.

Answers to the Parallelism Problem Set

1> **The correct answer is A.**
The verb " set " is in the base form to maintain the parallel structure with "monitor", as both are actions the software allows.

2> **The correct answer is C.**
The phrase "to give" ensures a parallel structure in the sentence, which means each part of the sentence follows the same grammatical pattern. The previous two verbs "practice" and "stay" are both preceded by "to", so following the same pattern for "give" improves the clarity and rhythm of the sentence.

3> **The correct answer is C.**
This choice uses a parallel structure, maintaining the pattern of noun phrases introduced by "in terms of". Each item in the list ("long-distance travel", "the availability of refueling infrastructure in many regions", and "the convenience of fast refueling options") follows the same format.

4> **The correct answer is C.**
This choice ensures a parallel structure, which improves the clarity of the sentence. The structure "not only for... but also for..." is a common way to express a comparison or contrast between two things. Here, it correctly compares "traditional film rolls" and "separate digital cameras".

5> **The correct answer is A.**
The verb "redirect" is in the base form to maintain the parallel structure with "stop", as both are actions Sarah decided to take.

6> **The correct answer is D.**
This choice maintains a parallel structure (a series of simple present tense verbs: decorate, purchase, and exchange) and clear, concise wording, making it the best option.

7> **The correct answer is C.**
The choice maintains the parallel structure by repeating "how they" before each verb phrase ("undergo evolutionary changes" and "interact with other organisms"). This consistent structure keeps the list coherent and easy to follow.

Answers to the Pronoun Agreement Problem Set

1> **The correct answer is A.**
It refers to the Greek Hellenistic period which is singular. Therefore, the possessive pronoun "its" is used to show that the sculptures were created during that particular period.

2> **The correct answer is B.**
The sentence refers to the United States as a singular entity, so the possessive pronoun "its" is appropriate to indicate that the United States must balance its own economic and political interests with moral and ethical responsibilities.

3> **The correct answer is C.**
The sentence refers to readers and their ability to examine and appreciate their own cultural heritage. The possessive pronoun "their" is appropriate in this context to indicate that readers have the opportunity to explore and appreciate their own cultural heritage through the lens provided by literature.

4> **The correct answer is A.**
The sentence refers to the principal of the school, who is making a decision about whether he or his brother would be the better candidate for the vacant teaching position. In this case, the subjective pronoun "he" is needed to complete the sentence.

5> **The correct answer is B.**
The sentence is describing a dolphin, which is a singular noun. The possessive pronoun "its" is used to indicate that the sleek and streamlined body belongs to the dolphin.

6> **The correct answer is B.**
The sentence is referring to the dishes of a specific restaurant, so the possessive pronoun "its" is appropriate to indicate that the restaurant advertised that its dishes were both healthy and delicious.

7> **The correct answer is B.**
The sentence is referring to the digestive system of giant pandas, which has adapted to their plant-based diet. The pronoun "it" is used to refer back to the digestive system as a singular noun.

8> **The correct answer is A.**
The sentence is referring to bonsai trees, which are plural, and describing their beauty and symbolism. The possessive pronoun "their" is appropriate to indicate that bonsai trees are highly prized for their beauty and symbolism.

9> **The correct answer is B.**
The sentence is referring to chopsticks, which is a plural noun. The pronoun "they" is appropriate to indicate that chopsticks were initially used for cooking and later adopted for use at the dining table.

10> **The correct answer is C.**
The sentence is referring to the speaker and their teammate. In this case, the objective pronoun "me" is needed after "and" to complete the sentence. It indicates that both the speaker and their teammate needed to commit to practicing regularly and focusing on refining their skills.

11> **The correct answer is D.**
The subordinating clause starts with the second-person perspective, and the main clause needs to use the same perspective, maintaining a direct, instructional tone.

Answers to the Subjunctive Mood Problem Set

1> **The correct answer is C.**
The sentence structure indicates that the HR manager is recommending an action to be taken after developing healthy cafeteria menus. The verb "recommend" is followed by the conjunction "that," which is commonly used to introduce a clause expressing a suggestion or recommendation.

2> **The correct answer is A.**
This is the correct answer. The sentence is expressing a hypothetical condition and its potential outcome in the past. The structure "Had + subject + past participle" is used to form a conditional sentence in the past perfect subjunctive mood.
In this case, the sentence suggests that Joseph could have achieved higher grades if he had been more diligent in his studies. The correct structure to convey this meaning is "Had Joseph been more diligent in his studies."

3> **The correct answer is A.**
The sentence is expressing advice given by doctors, and the verb "advised" is followed by the conjunction "that," which introduces a clause expressing advice or recommendation.
In this case, the doctors are advising that a cancer patient should make necessary lifestyle adjustments for better outcomes. The phrase "a cancer patient make necessary lifestyle adjustments" correctly conveys this meaning. The verb "make" is in the base form, which is used after the verb "advised" in this construction. The use of the present tense "make" suggests an ongoing action that the doctors are recommending the cancer patient to take for better outcomes.

4> **The correct answer is A.**
The sentence is expressing a hypothetical condition, using the subjunctive mood to indicate an unreal or unlikely situation. The phrase "If I were the president" sets up the hypothetical scenario.

5> **The correct answer is C.**
The sentence is expressing a hypothetical condition in the past. The use of the phrase "If they had listened to my advice" indicates an unrealized or unreal past situation.
In this case, the speaker is discussing the consequences of not following their advice. The phrase "they wouldn't be in this situation" implies that their current situation could have been avoided if they had listened to the advice. The correct structure to convey this meaning is "If they had listened to my advice."

6> **The correct answer is D.**
The sentence is expressing a hypothetical condition in the future. The phrase "If it should be sunny tomorrow" suggests a hypothetical situation where the weather is sunny the next day.
In this case, the speaker is discussing the possibility of going to the beach based on the condition of sunny weather. The phrase "we would go to the beach" indicates the hypothetical action that would occur if the condition is met.

Answers to the Transition Problem Set

1> **The correct answer is A) Afterward,**
The sentence describes a sequence of events. The first part states that the company's stock price plummeted following the announcement of a major data breach. The transition used to complete the text should logically connect this information to the next part, which mentions the CEO issuing a statement to reassure customers and outline steps the company was taking.

2> **The correct answer is B) As a result,**
The transition being tested is the logical consequence or result of the previous information. The phrase "As a result" connects the advancements in quantum computing and the ability of scientists to make groundbreaking discoveries at an unprecedented rate.

Choice A, "At the same time," doesn't provide a clear cause-and-effect relationship between the advancements in quantum computing and the groundbreaking discoveries. Choice C, "Similarly," suggests that there is a similarity between the advancements in quantum computing and something else, which is not stated in the given text. Choice D, "Instead," implies a contradiction or alternative scenario, which doesn't align with the information provided about the accelerated pace of scientific research.

3> **The correct answer is C) Similarly,**
The sentence describes efforts to promote women's suffrage in two different cities: New York and Chicago. The context shows that the methods in Chicago were comparable to those in New York in terms of their focus on raising awareness for the cause. Using "Similarly" provides a logical transition by highlighting the parallel efforts in both regions.

4> **The correct answer is A) Alternatively,**
The sentence presents two contrasting approaches to decision-making. It states that some people prefer to weigh the pros and cons before making a choice, while others may go with their gut instinct. The logical transition should introduce the alternative approach to decision-making mentioned in the second part.

5> **The correct answer is C) Afterward,**
The sentence describes a sequence of events. It states that the team struggled to find a breakthrough in their research, but after conducting further experiments and analyzing the data, they made an important discovery. The logical transition should connect this information to the next part, which mentions the team publishing their findings in a scientific journal.

6> **The correct answer is D) By the same token,**
The sentence presents a contrast between the benefits and drawbacks of virtual meetings. It states that virtual meetings can save time and money compared to in-person meetings, but they can also lack the personal connection and nonverbal cues. The logical transition should introduce the contrasting or balancing aspect of the second part.

7> **The correct answer is D) Accordingly,**
The transition "Accordingly" indicates that the actions taken by retailers mentioned in the second part of the sentence are a logical response or consequence of the increasing popularity of online shopping. It effectively connects the two parts of the sentence by showing that retailers are adapting to the trend of online shopping to provide a better experience for customers.

Answers to the Transition Problem Set (cont.)

8> **The correct answer is A) Finally,**
The sentence describes a sequence of events. It states that the film director spent years developing his script and scouting locations before filming began. The logical transition should connect this information to the next part, which mentions the premiere of the movie and its reception. supports or illustrates this point.

9> **The correct answer is A) For example,**
The sentence presents a continuation or addition to the information provided in the first part. It states that many countries build renewable energy infrastructure to reduce their dependence on fossil fuels. The logical transition should introduce an example that supports or illustrates this point.

10> **The correct answer is C) In addition,**
The transition being tested is the addition of further information. The phrase "In addition" connects the positive effects of physical exercise on mental health with the additional benefits it provides for overall physical well-being.

Choice A, "In contrast," suggests a comparison between the positive effects of physical exercise on mental health and something that has contrasting effects, which is not mentioned in the given text. Choice B, "For instance," introduces an example, which is not required in this context as the sentence already states the positive effects of physical exercise. Choice D, "Similarly," implies that there is a similarity between the positive effects of physical exercise on mental health and something else, which is not stated in the given text.

11> **The correct answer is B) Increasingly,**
It logically connects the rise of remote work and online learning with the proactive actions of companies and universities in exploring innovative ways to foster collaboration. It indicates that as remote work and online learning become more common, there's a growing trend of seeking new ways to engage virtual teams and students.

Option A) "At the same time," while not incorrect, is less precise as it suggests these activities are happening concurrently but not necessarily related. Option C) "Particularly," is not the best fit as it suggests that the following clause is a specific example of the preceding clause, which is not the case here. Option D) "Conversely," is incorrect as it suggests a contrast or contradiction between the two clauses, but the text presents an evolution or consequence, not a contrast.

12> **The correct answer is A) Indeed,**
The term "Indeed," is used in this context because it serves to emphasize or confirm a point that was just made. In the preceding sentence, the point is made that the company's revenue has been increasing over the past few years. The statement "it has nearly doubled since 2017" provides specific, emphatic evidence to support this point. Thus, "Indeed," serves as a transition that reinforces the point made in the first sentence. The other options either suggest a contrasting point (C) or an additional point (B and D), which are not applicable in this context where reinforcement is intended.

13> **The correct answer is B) Therefore,**
The sentence presents a cause-and-effect relationship. It states that the city has seen a significant increase in bike ridership over the past few years, and the logical transition should introduce the consequence or action that follows as a result of this trend.

Answers to the Transition Problem Set (cont.)

14> The correct answer is A) However,
The sentence presents a contrast or opposing viewpoint. It states that critics have dubbed Christopher Nolan the "master of mind-bending cinema" due to the complexity of his films' narratives and non-linear structures. The logical transition should introduce a contrasting or opposing statement made by Nolan himself.

15> The correct answer is C) To that end,
The phrase "To that end" is the most suitable transition in this context. It signifies the introduction of an action or event that is aligned with or serves the purpose stated in the first part of the sentence.

16> The correct answer is A) Still,
The sentence presents a contrast between the behavior of many people who have switched to online shopping during the pandemic and the preference of others for the traditional shopping experience. The logical transition should introduce the contrasting viewpoint or behavior.

17> The correct answer is B) However,
The sentence presents a contrasting viewpoint or argument. It states that while historians have called Marie Curie the "mother of modern physics" to recognize her groundbreaking work, some scientists argue against this nickname. The logical transition should introduce the opposing viewpoint or argument.

18> The correct answer is B) Nevertheless,
The sentence presents a contrast between the CEO's promise to increase salaries and benefits for employees and the board of directors vetoing the proposal. The logical transition should introduce a contrasting statement that acknowledges this contrast while highlighting the CEO's continued efforts.

19> The correct answer is A) On the other hand,
The sentence presents a contrast between the positive aspects of studying abroad and the potential challenges or drawbacks. The logical transition should introduce the opposing viewpoint or the contrasting information.

20> The correct answer is A) Namely,
The sentence presents a list of three favorite foods and the following statement explains that these are the foods that the person could eat every day without getting tired of them. The logical transition should introduce a clarifying statement or a more specific explanation.

21> The correct answer is A) Nevertheless,
The sentence presents a contrast between the athlete suffering a minor injury during training and her subsequent success in winning the competition and setting a new personal record. The logical transition should introduce a contrasting or opposing statement that highlights this contrast.

22> The correct answer is D) For example,
The sentence presents a continuation or addition to the information provided in the first part. It states that advances in technology have revolutionized many industries, including healthcare, transportation, and entertainment. The logical transition should introduce a specific example that supports or exemplifies this point.

Answers to the Transition Problem Set (cont.)

23> The correct answer is B) however,

The transition "however" is the most appropriate choice to complete the text. It signifies the introduction of a contrasting statement that contradicts or provides an opposing viewpoint to the initial plan of going to the beach. In this case, it connects the plan to go to the beach with the contradictory information from the weather forecast predicting thunderstorms. The use of "however" effectively conveys the change of circumstances or unexpected obstacle that alters the original plan.

24> The correct answer is B) Second,

The term "Second," is used in this context because it introduces another reason or point that supports the historian's claim that the castle was built for defensive purposes. In this case, the author is presenting a list of reasons or evidence. After stating the first point about the strategic location of the castle, "Second," logically transitions to the next point about the castle's thick stone walls and fortified towers. The other options don't provide this kind of continuity or sense of a sequence in presenting supporting points or evidence.

25> The correct answer is B) That said,

The phrase "That said" is appropriate here because it introduces a contrast between Aristotle's seemingly simple classification methods and the modern confirmation of their accuracy. Although Aristotle's approach might appear rudimentary compared to today's genetic analyses, his groupings have held up well, highlighting the validity of his observations. "That said" is commonly used to present a surprising or contrasting statement, making it the most logical and precise choice in this context.

Answers to the Dangling Modifier Problem Set

1> **The correct answer is A.**
The subject correctly does the action "discovering."

2> **The correct answer is A.**
Jane is the subject who was encouraged by one of her professors.

3> **The correct answer is D.**
The blue-ringed octopus is the one which is known to be highly venomous.

4> **The correct answer is C.**
The companies which offer a reasonable salary can attract employees.

5> **The correct answer is B.**
John is the one who disclosed his recent transaction.

6> **The correct answer is C.**
Lucy mixed Mentos and Coke, therefore the subject should be Lucy.

7> **The correct answer is A.**
Since the modifier says a representative, the subject has to be one person. Answer choice C makes the sentence a fragment.

Answers to the Boundaries Problem Set

1> **The correct answer is A.**
However cannot join two independent clauses.

2> **The correct answer is D.**
In this case, the term a natural ability to perceive and understand mathematical concepts is a type of appositive phrase, which is a noun or noun phrase that renames another noun right beside it. The appositive can be a short or long combination of words. In this sentence, a natural ability is an appositive for mathematical intuition.

3> **The correct answer is A.**
This choice allows the two independent clauses to be properly separated and provides the right punctuation for the transition word "while" at the beginning of the new sentence.

4> **The correct answer is C.**
In this case, the interplay is the subject and the verbs are underscores and highlights. Since the conjunction and joins only two verbs, no comma is needed before the conjunction and.

5> **The correct answer is A.**
There are two independent clauses joined by a coordinating conjunction so.

6> **The correct answer is B.**
The two periods in a modifying phrase(such as~) is joined by the conjunction and. The word influenced is used as a participle(adjective) in this sentence, so answer choice C makes it a run-on.

Answers to the Boundaries Problem Set (cont.)

7> **The correct answer is D.**
The answer is D, "warm; instead," because it properly separates two independent clauses. An independent clause is a group of words that contains a subject and verb and expresses a complete thought.

In this case, "they do not have a layer of blubber to keep them warm" and "they rely on their thick, waterproof fur to stay dry and insulated" are both independent clauses, each containing a subject ("they") and a verb ("do not have" and "rely").

The semicolon (;) is used to separate these two related yet independent thoughts. The word "instead" then serves as a transition between the two ideas, indicating a contrast.

8> **The correct answer is D.**
A period is needed to separate the two independent clauses.

9> **The correct answer is C.**
The sentence starts with a modifier, saying that from~ to~. Then there is a verb continues. To set off the modifier, a comma is needed before a subject.

10> **The correct answer is C.**
The phrase "with many scientific studies showing its potential benefits" correctly connects the subject "scientific studies" with the verb "showing".

This creates a modifying phrase that describes the studies and is grammatically and logically connected to the rest of the sentence. This phrasing doesn't create an independent clause, so it doesn't require additional punctuation like a comma or a period.

11> **The correct answer is A.**
In this case, the verb next to the blank is are which is plural. Answer choice C would not work because saying Henna is made and are ground is grammatically wrong. The plural verb are should be matched with the leaves(a plural noun).

12> **The correct answer is A.**
Here, we have two independent sentences and hence they are best separated by a period.

13> **The correct answer is B.**
Answer choices A and C makes run-on sentences. For answer choice D, there is a fragment after the semicolon. B separates two independent clauses.

14> **The correct answer is A.**
Here, "though" acts as a transitional phrase leading into a counterpoint. The colon (:) is used after "though" to introduce an explanation of the statement that precedes it. It is indeed correct to use a colon here, as it introduces a further explanation or elaboration of the point made in the first part of the sentence, that the most fascinating objects were not the most visually impressive.

Answers to the Rhetorical Synthesis Problem Set

1> **The correct answer is B.**
This option effectively addresses the disadvantage of using biological markers for predicting disease outbreaks. It clearly states the limitation—misidentification of markers due to genetic variability—and contrasts it with the reliability of models based on environmental factors.

2> **The correct answer is C.**
This choice effectively uses the given information to emphasize the relative sizes of the populations in Tokyo and Seoul. It addresses both the raw population numbers and the percentage of the total national population that each city represents, which provides a clearer picture of the demographic situation in each city.

The other options do not draw this specific comparison. Option A and B mainly state the information without providing a direct comparison between the population proportions in the two cities. Option D simply restates the data of the countries, not their capitals, without drawing any inferences or comparisons.

Answers to the Practice Test 1

1> **The correct answer is B.**
It uses the present tense, which is consistent with the preceding verbs "are watered" and "exposed." In the sentence, the seeds are currently being watered and exposed to light, and the next action is the germination of the seeds. "Germinate" is the appropriate verb form to indicate the ongoing process of seeds sprouting and beginning to grow.

2> **The correct answer is A.**
The sentence needs a main verb and the word usually indicates a common or typical behavior of wolves. The verb prefer implies that wolves have a natural inclination or choice to hunt smaller prey like rabbits and rodents.

3> **The correct answer is C.**
The relative pronoun refers to *a concept*, and C is the only singular verb.

4> **The correct answer is D.**
There are two clauses joined by a conjunction while.

5> **The correct answer is B.**
The participial phrase *"created by wildlife conservationists in South Africa"* should be either set off by commas to show it is a non-essential clause or omit the commas to show it is an essential clause. There can't be just a comma between a subject and a verb. For that reason alone, choice C and D can be eliminated. Also, you should see the participial phrase as a whole - the comma after *created* is unnecessary.

6> **The correct answer is A.**
It agrees with the singular subject "John Smith."

7> **The correct answer is A.**
The sentence starts with the modifier since discovering, and the subject needs to be the one who discovered.

8> The correct answer is A.

There are two clauses.

Marine biologist Emily Wong recently explored the Reef to study its diverse marine life.

The reef is home to over 600 types of coral and thousands of species of fish.

And a modifier ***spanning over 2,300 kilo¬meters*** is in the middle of these two clauses. In this context, the spanning is not modifying the marine life. Rather, it modifies the reef. Answer choices B and D do not work. The answer choice C may seem right, but there is no comma before the coordinating conjunction ***and***.

9> The correct answer is B.

Calcium oxide is a restrictive appositive; therefore, no comma is needed around it. When the information goes from general to specific, it is usually a restrictive appositive; the opposite is true for a nonrestrictive appositive.

10> The correct answer is A.

To that end is a phrase commonly used to introduce a statement or action that is intended to achieve a particular goal or objective. In this case, the goal is to improve employee morale, and the action being taken is planning a company retreat. Using the phrase To that end clearly indicates that the company retreat is being organized with the specific purpose of building teamwork and fostering positive relationships among the staff, which aligns with the goal of improving employee morale.

11> The correct answer is C.

The phrase "In addition" is used to introduce additional information, which fits well with the context of the sentence. It effectively conveys that there is another noteworthy feature or facility that the science center offers. It's a smooth and natural way to continue the description and maintain the flow of the text.

12> The correct answer is A.

The word "therefore" is used to indicate a logical consequence or conclusion based on the information provided in the first sentence. In this case, the first sentence states that the widespread use of disposable plastic products has led to an environmental crisis. The word "therefore" connects this cause-and-effect relationship and implies that as a result of this crisis, many governments and companies are now taking steps to reduce plastic waste.

13> The correct answer is A.

This option emphasizes the difference in the focus of the two inventions: Edison's light bulb transformed everyday life and safety, while the Wright brothers' airplane revolutionized transportation. It aligns well with the student's goal of highlighting a clear distinction.

B) Discusses the groundbreaking nature of both inventions but fails to emphasize their specific differences.
C) Lists the years of the inventions but does not highlight how they differ.
D) Mentions the contributions but doesn't clearly define their contrasting focuses.

14> The correct answer is B.

This choice most effectively utilizes the relevant information from the notes to describe the study and its methodology. It includes the problem being investigated (understanding how sea turtles save energy), the researcher who conducted the study (Adriana Zavala), and the methodology used (computer modeling to examine the effect of ocean currents).

Answers to the Practice Test 1 (cont.)

15> **The correct answer is B.**
This choice provides a generalization about the Korean Wave, effectively summarizing its global cultural influence, economic impact, and the role of government support as mentioned in the notes.

A) While it highlights the popularity of K-pop, it focuses on a specific aspect (music) rather than making a broader generalization about the Korean Wave as a whole.
C) This choice discusses the global appeal of South Korean television dramas but does not generalize about the entire Korean Wave.
D) Although it mentions the role of government sponsorship, it focuses on a specific factor rather than providing a comprehensive generalization about the Korean Wave.

Answers to the Practice Test 2

1> **The correct answer is A.**
The sentence lacks a verb and the subject is people which is plural.

2> **The correct answer is C.**
The sentence contains two clauses with the subordinating conjunction while.

3> **The correct answer is B.**
The sentence is referring to a specific event that happened in the past when William Hanna and Joseph Barbera created their first cartoon series, Tom and Jerry. Therefore, the past tense "launched" is the appropriate verb form to use.

4> **The correct answer is A.**
The phrase developing mobile X-ray units for use on the front lines of World War I and training medical professionals in their use is used to provide further information about her contributions.

5> **The correct answer is A.**
The sentence starts with a modifier that describes the subject. In this case, the critics are the people who do the analysis.

6> **The correct answer is C.**
The main subject of the sentence is "speculation," and the main verb is "is." Adding another finite verb in the blank (e.g., "maintains") would result in a clause with one subject and two verbs without a conjunction, which is grammatically incorrect. To avoid this error, a participial phrase ("maintaining") is used instead. This creates a grammatically correct structure by describing the speculation without introducing a second finite verb.

Answers to the Practice Test 2 (cont.)

7> **The correct answer is C.**
The phrase majestic giants reaching towards the sky is a nonrestrictive appositive that needs to be framed with two commas or the em-dashes. In this case, the em dash is shown before the word majestic, so another em dash is needed.

8> **The correct answer is D.**
The such as phrase is a restrictive phrase that modifies features. Colons should not be used before or after such as. Although regarding the phrase as restrictive or nonrestrictive is subjective – meaning there could be a comma before such as – a comma is wrongly placed after such as in answer choice C.

9> **The correct answer is B.**
A semicolon is used for the listing, and the listing follows the parallelism rule.

10> **The correct answer is A.**
Through which is a conjunction that joins the main clause "Scientists put forth the hypothesis that dolphins engage in cooperative play, a deliberate, repeated, and interactive behavior" and the subordinating clause "these intelligent marine mammals strengthen social bonds, refine their communication skills, and enhance their cognitive abilities"

11> **The correct answer is A.**
It effectively connects the two statements and indicates a logical consequence or conclusion. The word "Therefore" signals that the information that follows is a result or implication of the previous statement. In this case, it indicates that because lack of sleep can have negative impacts on physical and mental health, schools and employers are starting to prioritize healthy sleep habits. This choice creates a logical and coherent flow in the sentence, highlighting the cause-and-effect relationship between the two ideas.

12> **The correct answer is D.**
It effectively indicates the chronological sequence of events. "Afterward" suggests that the action of speaking to reporters took place following the completion of the race. This choice provides a clear and logical transition between the two sentences, indicating the subsequent event that occurred.

13> **The correct answer is D.**
Its statement brings out a common theme between the two books -- they both portray growth and learning experiences. This is a direct comparison of the two works and effectively highlights their similarity. Other choices make either incorrect comparisons or don't focus on the similarity between the two books.

14> **The correct answer is A.**
The goal here is to highlight the objective of the research study. The best choice would be option A, which summarizes the objective to understand factors influencing amphibian hibernation, a topic less studied compared to its mammalian counterparts.

15> **The correct answer is D.**
The goal of the student is to emphasize a difference between yeast and sourdough starter. Option D does this most effectively by stating the different requirements of the two rising agents to produce carbon dioxide.

Answers to the Practice Test 3

1> **The correct answer is D.**
In this sentence, we are referring to the estimations of travel agents. To indicate possession or ownership by multiple travel agents, we use the plural form "agents" followed by an apostrophe ('), denoting that the estimations belong to the travel agents.

2> **The correct answer is choice D.**
The conjunction and is used to list the actions of the infinitives: communicate, access, and perform.

3> **The correct answer is C.**
The relative pronoun conjunction *that* refers to the plural nouns: products and solutions.
Therefore, it needs a plural verb.

4> **The correct answer is A.**
The phrase tons of them is an unrestrictive phrase that modifies features. Since there is an em dash to set off the phrase, the other side needs an em dash too.

5> **The correct answer is D.**
The prepositional phrase in 1801 conveys the past.

6> **The correct answer is D.**
The sentence starts with the subordinating conjunction while and contains only two clauses.

7> **The correct answer is C.**
Since the sentence starts with modifier, the subject should do the juggling.

8> **The correct answer is B.**
The conjunctive adverb however cannot connect the two clauses physically, so answer choice C and D cannot be correct. It emphasizes the contrast or contradiction between the lack of thinking or decision-making abilities in machines and the envisioned future where machines can exhibit advanced cognitive capabilities. Therefore, however should be in the second sentence.

9> **The correct answer is A.**
"With this in mind" logically connects the identification of critical impurities with the decision to postpone the product release, signaling that the delay is a direct response to the issue mentioned.

10> **The correct answer is D.**
"That said" is correct because it introduces a contrasting perspective to the concerns raised in the first sentence.

11> **The correct answer is B.**
It effectively connects the sentence by indicating that Harriet Tubman's goal of eradicating slavery and promoting equality led her to actively participate in the Underground Railroad. The phrase "To that end" emphasizes her commitment and purpose in risking her safety to guide enslaved individuals to freedom. It creates a logical and coherent flow in the sentence, highlighting the connection between her beliefs and her actions.

Answers to the Practice Test 3 (cont.)

12> The correct answer is A.
It introduces an example or specific illustration to support the previous statement.
The phrase "For instance" effectively signals that the following statement will provide a specific example of a technological innovation that has become a part of everyday life. In this case, the example given is smartphones being commonly used for various purposes beyond communication.

13> The correct answer is B.
This option presents both the study and its methodology, describing Dr. Patel's focus on using climate models to understand the cooling effect of transpiration, which is the main point in the notes.

14> The correct answer is C.
The student's goal is to introduce Nilsson's research to an unfamiliar audience. Answer choice C provides a brief background of the Great Pyramid and introduces Nilsson's application of Lidar technology, which revealed previously unknown features within the pyramid.

15> The correct answer is B.
This option directly addresses the origin of the word "cheongsam" by explaining its meaning in Cantonese ("long shirt") and providing context about its cultural background.
A) Focuses on the dress's style and cultural elements but does not explain the word's origin.
C) Highlights its popularity but ignores the word's meaning.
D) Discusses the dress's timeline and popularity without addressing its name.

Answers to the Practice Test 4

1> The correct answer is D.
Species functions both as a singular and a plural word, so the apostrophe should be placed after *s*. In other words, the singular form of *species* is not *specie*. On top of that, the possessive form "'s" or "s'" is used to denote ownership or a characteristic of a noun. Here, you want to say the diversity of the species, not the diversity of the diversity of the species. The extra "'s" in "diversity's" in option A is superfluous and doesn't add anything to the meaning of the sentence.

2> The correct answer is B.
In this context, "its" is the correct choice because it's the possessive pronoun that refers to "the glue."

3> The correct answer is C.
The sentence needs a verb.

4> The correct answer is A.
The commas are used to list 3 verbs: secure, manage, and ensure. The later commas are used to list the objects of the verb ensure.

5> The correct answer is A.
Laying(a participial phrase) shows an action that succeeds the first clause. Since *laying* does not modify *exploration*, B is wrong. There is no independent clause after *laying*, so C and D are also wrong.

Answers to the Practice Test 4 (cont.)

6> The correct answer is A.
The sentence starts with a modifier that shows the action of the subject. The subject should be someone/something that does the *conducting*, and it is the economists.

7> The correct answer is C.
It needs to modify the *view* of *AI*. Changing to *portraying* makes the modifying clause *portraying it as a threat to human employment* becomes ambiguous. It may modify not only the *view* of *AI* but also *Dr. Kim*. Therefore, A is wrong answer. Answer choices B and D makes the sentence run-on.

8> The correct answer is D.
The subject is the noun clause that starts with *How*, and the main verb is *is*. There is a nonessential modifier inferred by the first comma after adversity, so you need another comma to set off the modifier.

9> The correct answer is D.
The colon further describes what the two exams are. B and C are incorrect because there is no independent clause after *exams*. A is not correct because the sentence does not express an action that occurs when the applicants must pass two exams.

10> The correct answer is C.
The word "increasingly" indicates a growing trend or shift towards a certain behavior or practice. In this case, it suggests that more and more employers are starting to implement programs to support the mental health of their employees and reduce the stigma surrounding mental illness.

11> The correct answer is B.
The word "therefore" is used to indicate a logical consequence or conclusion based on the preceding statement or situation. In this case, the preceding statement mentions the effects of climate change leading to more frequent and severe flooding in coastal communities. The word "therefore" suggests that as a result of this situation, architects and city planners are designing buildings and infrastructure to withstand rising sea levels and storms. It implies a cause-and-effect relationship, where the effects of climate change lead to a specific action being taken.

12> The correct answer is A.
Additionally is used to introduce an additional point or piece of information that supports or expands upon the initial statement. In this case, it signifies that there is another factor contributing to Japan's secure borders, following the mention of its geographical location.

13> The correct answer is D.
This choice highlights the role of The Travels of Marco Polo in inspiring Columbus's journey, which, due to the misconception about Asia's location, resulted in the discovery of the Americas. This effectively captures how the misconception about Asia's proximity led to the exploration of new territories.

14> The correct answer is B.
It effectively emphasizes the similarity between the two survival strategies of the Arctic fox: both involve scavenging. It clearly connects the behavior of following polar bears and rummaging through human garbage as two comparable methods of finding food.

15> The correct answer is C.
It specifically mentions the time period of their work, which is the early 1990s, and highlights their efforts to protect Ainu culture through the establishment of the Ainu Museums in Nibutani and Chitose.
It effectively uses relevant information from the notes to emphasize the length and purpose of their work.